SCHOLARS, SAINTS AND SINNERS

Also by Chris Armstrong

Anything from a Pin to an Elephant (Amberley), 2016
Mustard, Boots and Beer (Larks Press), 2014
Under the Parson's Nose (Larks Press), 2012

Scholars, Saints and Sinners

the stories of some of Norfolk's more idiosyncratic clergy of the

19ᵗʰ and early 20ᵗʰ centuries

Chris Armstrong

POPPYLAND
PUBLISHING

Designed and typeset in 12 on 14 pt Gilamesh Pro

Printed by Ashford Colour Press

Picture credits:

Archant, 99
Author's collection, 42, 86, 131, 132
Kolforn (cc-by-sa/4.0), cover, 96
Inkedmik (cc-by-sa/2.0), 93
Museum of Army Chaplaincy, 126, 136
Norfolk Record Office (DN/ADR/15/8/9/3) — 66, 74, 75, (MC1983) —90, 97
Norwich School, 50
Page M, 61
Picture Norfolk (NCC), 129
Poppyland collection, 42, 119, 124
Public domain, 146
Wikimedia commons, 54

Contents

List of illustrations

Preface

A while ago a friend who had read my books on Norwich entrepreneurs and Norfolk department stores asked me why I hadn't written a book about the 'family business'. He was referring to the Church. That I was the son of a Norfolk parson (last parish St Margaret's, King's Lynn), the grandson of two more (paternal Heydon, maternal Salle) the great grandson of another (East Dereham), not to mention the great grandson and great-great-great grandson of other, non-Norfolk clerics, as well as the nephew of two more, and the cousin of an Archdeacon seemed to him to qualify me for the task! While being the son (and more) of the manse is really no qualification at all for such a task, the Church, and especially its personalities, have long interested me, and so I was tempted to take up the challenge.

When I was a child the house always seemed to be awash with dog collars as a succession of Curates, Vicars, Rural Deans, Canons and even the occasional Bishop dropped in for tea or coffee. So it is perhaps no surprise that, as a teenager, I became mildly addicted to Trollope—there are worse addictions for a teenager. Many years ago I was deputed to host, at a corporate dinner, a guest who had travelled widely with Macmillan when he was Prime Minister. When I asked him about Supermac's legendary calm he told me that whenever Macmillan felt under stress he would retire for an hour and read from Trollope, emerging with the calmest of demeanours. I've tried it and I can recommend this therapy to anyone. Looking at the characters of some Victorian clergy it is often tempting to define them by the parallels with their fictional Barsetshire counterparts, though happily my research for this book didn't turn up anyone quite as odious as Obadiah Slope, even if one or two came near.

This book does not restrict itself just to the Victorian era, but it is not surprising that many of the more interesting characters do come from that time. Susanna Wade Martins, in a piece for *Rural History Today*, written in 2015, reviews the position of the rural parson in those days, describing as typical 'an educated and well-connected gentleman who cared deeply about the spiritual health of his flock, tried to improve church attendance, resisted non-conformity and played a pivotal role in developing education and the care of the poor'. She goes on to make the point that the role could be lonely, with the parson not being entirely at ease either with the Squirearchy or the farmers because of the disparity in the one case of income, and the other of education.

Not all of course suffered this loneliness and some were far from poor. In his diary my great grandfather made frequent reference to one neighbouring parson who not only owned a vineyard in South Africa but spent all week at his office in London. Not that he disliked the man, in fact he tartly described him as 'being admirable in all matters not connected with his profession'. But it was far more likely, as we emerged from the period of pluralities, when curates were paid very little to do all the work for a non-resident incumbent, that local clergy themselves could feel this detachment from the Squire, because of an inadequate stipend. By the mid nineteenth century almost all those who were ordained were Oxbridge graduates and thus detached by education and interest from their yeoman neighbours. It is not therefore surprising that some rural clergy pursued intellectual pursuits, sometimes to the point of eccentricity.

Norfolk offers several examples, particularly literary ones, of parsons with the inclination to follow intellectual pursuits, and the leisure with which to do so. Particularly interesting examples covered in this book are the eccentric Revd Elwin of Booton, though as a 'Squarson' he hardly qualifies for sympathy on financial grounds and the remarkable Augustus Jessopp of Scarning, one-time Headmaster of Norwich Grammar School.

The parsons discussed in this book are a diverse group. They range from the intellectually inclined Jessopp and Elwin, through the church builders and improvers— Marcon and Elwin again and the heroic George Smith at Rorke's Drift, to the eccentric Davidson of Stiffkey and the outrageous Loftus, who hired two prostitutes to act as domestic servants—their less domestic charms being shared indiscriminately between Loftus and his manservant.

During the Victorian era, the role of the parson changed dramatically and still changes. For the Church in the nineteenth century the schism between the evangelicals and the followers of the Oxford Movement was real. The growth of non-conformism and the development of Darwinian thinking were real threats, as was, in the countryside, agricultural depression.

The high regard in which some clergy had been held as leaders of the local community, sometimes in an uneasy relationship with the Squire, was being challenged too. Their authority was gradually losing a tug of war with outside influences as communication and travel opened minds and opportunities. Even so, right up to the

Great War some semblance of their influential position was visible, even if mainly to their own eyes. Thus, my grandfather began his annual letter in 1913 to his then North Tuddenham parishioners by writing that 'politics has no place in a communication between parson and parishioners'. It didn't however stop him, in the same letter, from castigating 'artizans' (sic) for 'flaring up' into unrest 'on the slightest excuse' and 'politically-minded women' (suffragettes) for indulging in 'unchecked outrages'. He used his 1915 letter to criticise those young single men in the parish who had not yet volunteered for the army, telling them that even a late decision to do so would allow them at least a 'tarnished' honour which they would be denied if they waited for conscription. Parsons probably forewent their influential positions in the community with regret.

The selection of candidates to include in this book presented quite a challenge. Some of the subjects are widely known but most are not. One of the frustrations of researching has been that in respect of some of the most promising candidates there has turned out to be insufficient material to justify a full chapter, and I have gathered some of these together in a series of brief essays as a final chapter.

My purpose has not been to write comprehensive biographies of the clergy covered. Sometimes a particular incident or characteristic is the only real point of general interest in their lives. In other cases a brief review of their origins and careers is more appropriate. As to into which category—Scholars, Saints or Sinners—each individual should be placed, I would suggest that Elwin and Jessopp clearly belong in the file marked 'Scholars'. Canonization is a long way beyond my remit and the perception of what constitutes 'sin' is, these days, so elastic as to be a matter of individual opinion, so I leave it to the reader to determine the appropriate category in respect of the other characters.

Acknowledgements

Researching for this book was rather like a mystery tour; so many of the characters, while well known in their time, have since drifted out of public consciousness. While I have not given detailed references for every source, I think it only fair to the reader who may wish to follow up on any of these stories to give a few clues!

Clearly the books listed in the Bibliography are a good starting point, and I would particularly draw attention to Karilyn Collier's privately published book on Harold Davidson, Rector of Stiffkey, of whom she is a direct descendant. I only became aware of it when I was lent a copy by an acquaintance who knew of my interest in the case, but I have since become aware that it can be bought online (www.rectorofstiffkey.co.uk). One interesting aspect of this book is that it provides an entirely different view of the Rector from that advanced, for example, by Matthew Parris. It is a very spirited defence of Davidson, written by his granddaughter, whose distress at what she sees as a great injustice is clear, and it should be read with that in mind. My own reservations about his conviction are founded mainly on the evidence of the trial transcripts, but in the interests of balance her side of the story needs to be heard as well.

Of the other books listed there I would particularly draw attention to Nick Hartley's biography of Augustus Jessopp. Again, there is a (more distant) family relationship between author and subject but it is a meticulously researched work and is full of clues as to where to look next. The website of the Dereham Antiquarian Society enables access to the newsletters of a local society set up especially to celebrate the work of Jessopp, and is well worth following up.

The Norfolk Record Office is an asset to be treasured. Without the resources there it would have been impossible to write this book, and without the help of the dedicated archivists there it would have taken a great deal longer. The online catalogue is a good start, but the knowledge of the staff at the Record Office is an enormous help when looking for original material. The records held there made a contribution to almost all the chapters in this book, but were especially helpful on Berney, Davidson, Marcon, Elwin and Holmes.

Some elements of research are so much easier these days because of the internet. In particular the British Library's Newspaper Archive and The Times Digital Archive are rich sources of contemporary views of individual incidents, but, as usual with press reports, one has to take care to consider the level of accuracy. The online archive of the Spectator is another source and all these archives sometimes give clues to the sort of anecdotes which I believe help to bring to life some of the characters being researched.

I would also like to acknowledge the help given by Cheryl Wood, the Librarian in charge of Archives at Norwich School, in making records available to me, and by Susanna and Peter Wade Martins who loaned me material about the Norfolk County School.

Chris Armstrong
Wroxham
March 2019

You may say what you like when you are in your proper place, the pulpit, but when you are in a court of justice, you must conform to the rules of that court.

A judicial put down to The Revd Berney on one of his many court appearances.

Revd Thomas Berney

Lord of the Manor, Rector of Bracon Ash, eccentric and compulsive litigant, charged in 1866 with having, by 'lewd and incontinent conversation and otherwise, solicited the chastity of two ladies'—the wife and sister-in-law of a neighbouring clergyman.

On Saturday 5 April 1856 *The Norfolk Chronicle* reported that 'on Tuesday last The Revd Thomas Berney MA was instituted to the Rectory of Bracon Ash in Norfolk on the presentation of Thomas Trench Berney Esq and Geo. Duckett Berney Esq, Trustees under the will of Elizabeth Berney, of Bracon Ash, spinster, deceased.'

Thomas was the second son of Thomas Trench Berney, the younger brother of Geo. Duckett Berney, and the nephew of Elizabeth Berney. Thus was provision made for the second son of many an old family, Thomas Berney was not the only subject in this book to benefit from family patronage. The Berneys were an ancient and distinguished family, whose motto was *Nil timere neque timore*, which translates as 'Nothing rashly, nor with fear'. The Revd Thomas certainly seems on occasion to have paid scant heed to the first half of the motto, at least.

After his institution Berney decided to live in Bracon Hall which along with other extensive property in the parish had been left to him by his Aunt Elizabeth. This meant that Bracon Rectory was untenanted and in 1860 it was let to the Rector of the neighbouring East Carleton, for whom suitable accommodation could not be found in his own parish. The Revd Cumming and his wife moved in and had their first child there, in 1862.

With only a small parish to occupy him, Berney developed other interests. As with others in his family before him he was a serious collector of majolica; some of his collection was sold at Sotheby's in 1946 and one piece, dating from 1532, was subsequently bequeathed to the Fitzwilliam Museum in Cambridge. Another which fetched, in 1973, a record price at the time of over £24,000 was sold by Christie's despite having a crack, the damage reported to have occurred when The Revd Berney's coach overturned en route to London taking the piece for an exhibition in 1862. His other interests included gardening and water colours.

His early relationship with his tenants at the Rectory seems to have been amicable. A shared interest with Mrs Cumming (Helen) in gardening was discovered and landlord and tenants were on friendly terms, with picnics in the 200 acre park attached to the Hall being a feature of the first few summers. Berney, a bachelor, was a frequent supper guest at the Rectory, though The Revd Cumming was to suggest later that this was simply a matter of good manners rather than genuine hospitality, as Berney often contrived to spin out his calls there until the meal was announced.

In the spring of 1864 Mrs Cumming's younger sister Maria Elizabeth, known as Bessie, came on an extended visit and was introduced to Berney. Both she and the Cumming continued to enjoy picnics with Berney, and sometimes dined at the Hall.

In mid-June, Bessie told her sister that she did not wish to be left alone with Berney again, explaining that, in late May, when Helen Cumming had been resting, sitting outside in the garden at the Hall, Berney had invited Bessie into his greenhouse to admire the spring flowers. Once there he had put his arm round her waist and kissed her against her will, before inviting her upstairs, an invitation she had declined. Two weeks later, indeed that very afternoon, she had been alone with him in the dining room at the Rectory and he had again tried to kiss her, only desisting when she threatened to scream.

Mrs Cumming immediately told the story to her husband and, for good measure, told him that she too had been importuned by Berney in a most unseemly manner. A month earlier Berney had visited the Rectory when her husband and sister had been out, ostensibly to paint flowers. Finding her alone he had invited her to join him on the sofa for 'a liaison between us', encouraging her by pointing out that with the blinds drawn they would not be seen. Helen said that she had been greatly shocked and threatened to tell her husband if he did not stop. She said that Berney had confidently expressed the view that she would not report him. Soon after the incident Berney had gone to stay with his family but as soon as he had returned he had got up to his old tricks again.

This time she had been alone with him in the drawing room. She was later to tell the court that he put his hand on her knee and—to quote her evidence—said:

> I want something very bad, I have been so excited all week. Do let me have my own way, a slice of a cut cake will never be missed. I shall go crazy if you don't let me have my own way.

He then implied that, if she declined, he would have to make do with one of the domestic staff at the Hall. She had made him promise not to behave in the same way again and told him that she would report the matter to her husband. But she didn't, not at least until the second incident with Bessie—about three weeks later.

Revd Cumming promptly wrote a letter of protest to Berney. Unfortunately there is no record of exactly what he wrote, but, not getting an immediate reply, he reported the matter to the Bishop. When he returned from his visit to Norwich to report the matter, Cumming found a reply from Berney waiting for him. It was a somewhat half-hearted apology, written in rather bizarre terms. Berney wrote that where two people met regularly together 'in mirth and fun' he felt that 'some latitude' was allowed. Whether this was meant to be a justification for flirting (and more) with Mrs Cumming is debatable but it certainly didn't go down well with her husband. The letter went on to apologise in apparent sincerity for any offence that might have been taken.

The Bishop reacted to Revd Cumming's complaint by immediately setting up an enquiry to investigate the matter. The panel comprised his Vicar General (effectively his deputy), the Archdeacon, three other clergymen and one layman. This preliminary investigation was able to interview possible witnesses, as was a lawyer acting for Berney. The panel concluded that there was a case to answer and the case was referred to the ecclesiastical court, the Court of Arches. In due course Berney was charged with 'soliciting the chastity' of both Helen and Bessie.

The mills of God grind slow, but they grind exceeding fine, goes the proverb. The Court of Arches has at least its pace in common with the mills of God. By the time the case came to court it was 12 May 1866, nearly two years after the alleged offences. During the intervening period there been several representations made to the Court on Berney's behalf seeking additional information from the Bishop. As the Bishop's only personal knowledge of the case was the original complaint made directly to him by The Revd Cumming there was very little he could add.

The set of dramatis personae for the case was an intriguing one, with a number of the principals having interesting backgrounds. The Judge was Dr Stephen Lushington, Dean of the Court of Arches. Lushington was the son of a baronet, an Old Etonian, and a Fellow of All Souls, Oxford. At the age of 24 he had been called to the Bar and entered Parliament in the Whig cause, as member for Great Yarmouth. It was only a brief spell in Parliament, but he was a lifelong supporter of the anti-slavery campaign and an early advocate of the abolition of the death penalty. Returning to the Bar he concentrated on building up a successful practice, acting amongst others for Lady Byron in her separation proceedings from the poet. But he subsequently sat in Parliament again for several constituencies including Tower Hamlets, a constituency which if it still existed as a single entity would probably today be about as likely to return an Oxonian Old Etonian as an orangutan on stilts. By 1866 he was 84 years old and had been a judge for nearly 30 years. The following year he retired on ill health grounds.

The Bishop was primarily represented by Dr Deane, QC, later Sir James Deane, who, having previously been Queen's Advocate (effectively legal adviser to the Foreign Office) became involved in some of the most important ecclesiastical cases of the period during which high church clergy were prosecuted, and in some cases jailed, for practices involving the restoration of ritual in the services of the church.

Berney's principal representative was Dr Travers Twiss, QC, later Sir Travers Twiss, who was certainly acquainted with Dr Deane, having succeeded him a few years earlier as Chancellor of the Diocese of London. Like Deane he had an established practice in the ecclesiastical courts and had also been greatly involved in international law. Ironically, he and his wife were, six years later, to be involved in another court case involving alleged sexual misconduct, this time by Lady Twiss, prior to their marriage. The couple brought a case for malicious libel with intent to extort. Unfortunately for them, as Lady Twiss could not cope with the prospect of cross examination, the case collapsed and within a week Twiss had resigned.

The proceedings opened with a request from Dr Deane for a delayed start since he had had a communication from Dr Twiss, and he hoped it might prove possible after a brief consultation to settle the matter without further ado. Whatever the content of the consultation it resolved nothing as it transpired that Dr Deane had been mistaken as to the source of the request, and the case opened. The evidence given in court focussed primarily on the prosecution, the arcane rules of the court at that time denying Berney the right to give evidence in person. The prosecution evidence comprised that of The Revd Cumming, Helen Cumming and Bessie. Both ladies were examined and cross-examined at length, in Helen's case for more than three hours. The evidence they gave was consistent with the story as set out above. In his cross-examination Dr Twiss questioned Helen about a letter she had written to Berney on 16 May between the two occasions on which she alleged he had acted improperly towards her. This letter had been in the kindest terms, thanking him for a gift, commenting on the fine weather and finishing with an assurance of the kind regards of herself, her husband, and Bessie.

Dr Lushington may have been 84, but he was obviously a man of stamina. Because of the delay at the start of the proceedings, and the length of the cross examination of Helen, it was already 4 o'clock when she finished giving evidence and Dr Deane proposed an adjournment. Lushington was having none of it and, although Bessie's ordeal in the box was shorter than Helen's, it was already approaching six o'clock when her evidence was concluded. Dr Twiss then asked whether, for convenience, it would be possible to hear the evidence of one defence witness, Mr Dye, the Parish Clerk, which was likely to take just five minutes and Dr Lushington concurred.

Mr Dye had been called because both ladies had agreed, during cross-examination, that, on Trinity Sunday, the day following the second alleged attempted seduction of Helen, they had received communion in Bracon Ash church. When asked why they had been willing to receive the sacrament from Berney, they both averred that, though Berney was in the congregation, he had not been officiating. Mr Dye claimed that Berney had been the celebrant. Presumably Twiss introduced this issue because, first, the willingness to accept the sacrament from Berney seemed inconsistent with Helen's reaction to his alleged behaviour the day before, and second because the question of who was the celebrant might cast doubt on the truthfulness of their evidence.

Following the conclusion of Mr Dye's evidence the case was adjourned until the following Monday, when it was the turn of The Revd Cumming to give evidence; he could add little to that already given by his wife and sister-in-law.

The procedures and rules of the court de-barring Berney from giving evidence, the principal defence witnesses called, other than the churchwarden, who confirmed Mr Dye's testimony, were servants from both the Rectory and the Hall, all of whom testified that they had witnessed no impropriety. As was the tradition in those days a few witnesses were also called to attest that the alleged behaviour was totally inconsistent with Berney's character.

In closing the case for the prosecution Dr Deane suggested that Berney might have tampered with the evidence, by offering financial inducements to those defence witnesses who were his tenants. He sought to explain Helen's original failure to complain to her husband after Berney's alleged advances by suggesting that she might have wished to avoid any unpleasantness, though he agreed it might have been better if she had done so. He justified her later decision to tell her husband as being a result of her concern about the liberties which Berney had subsequently taken with her younger sister for whose reputation she was concerned. He maintained that the charges were fully proved. This time, Dr Lushington, perhaps anticipating that Dr Twiss would not be brief, did not encourage a late sitting, adjourning the case without specifying a future hearing date, as the courts were so busy.

It was a further two weeks, on 28 May, before the case resumed. Dr Twiss spoke for about three hours. The line he took was predictable. There was no corroboration of the story of either lady, and Berney's letter of apology was no admission of guilt. He went on to refer to a precedent, a case in which the uncorroborated story of the victim of an alleged sexual assault had meant that the judge had felt unable to find the accused clergyman guilty. He forbore to mention that Lushington had also been the judge in that case. He ended by suggesting that the two ladies had made 'an exaggerated and distorted statement'.

Dr Deane responded. While accepting that the stories were uncorroborated he asked the judge to consider what motive they could possibly have for concocting such a story against someone with whom they had been on friendly terms. It would be a 'vile scheme'.

In his judgement Dr Lushington rejected the precedent suggested by Twiss as having no bearing on the case. He regarded the evidence of the two ladies as being mutually corroborative, and his observation of their demeanour when giving evidence gave him confidence that they were being truthful. Helen's failure to report the earlier incidents to her husband was a matter he had considered but he did not feel it weighed against her credibility as a witness. As for receiving the sacrament on Trinity Sunday, both ladies had averred that the mass was not celebrated by Berney. Even if it had been, though a more courageous lady might have declined to make communion, it did not change his view of her veracity. In short, he concluded that the case was substantially proved, and sentenced Berney to a two-year suspension from his office, and made an order for the costs to be borne by him.

Dr Twiss immediately gave notice of appeal to the Privy Council. The appeal was heard the following February; the verdict was overturned and Berney's suspension was lifted. The appeal decision suggests that the Privy Council took a different view from Dr Lushington on various issues. They felt that, without corroboration, it was dangerous to rely so much on Mrs Cumming's recollection of the exact words, perhaps she had misunderstood what Berney had meant. They had reservations about the probability of

Berney having proposed immediate adultery in a room where interruption was quite possible, and they felt that Mrs Cumming's subsequent behaviour, writing in friendly terms, meeting for picnics, accepting gifts and dinner invitations, would have been an inappropriate and unlikely sequel to the behaviour of which she complained. As far as Bessie was concerned, she was a single lady and there was no impropriety in Berney having made advances to her.

Perhaps it was also in the minds of the members of the Council that it seemed strange that, given their alleged previous experiences, both ladies allowed themselves to be left alone with Berney again, and that Mrs Cumming had not been minded to tell her husband of the advances until she discovered that she was not the only object of Berney's attention.

Curiously while all this drama was playing out The Revd Berney continued to act out his role as Lord of the Manor. Just a week after the guilty verdict he hosted what the press described as 'a substantial dinner and tea' for his parishioners on the lawn at Bracon Hall, with transport provided for all those who could not walk, and an evening display of fireworks, after which the health of the Rector was proposed and the entire company sang the National Anthem 'loyally and heartily'. It seems safe to assume that the Cummings and Bessie didn't attend. They had, by then, moved out of the Rectory. The local press sententiously opined that such gatherings tended to 'produce the good feelings of the sons and daughters of the toil towards their superiors'!

Berney's character was clearly not permanently damaged—he was a guest at a Buckingham Palace 'Drawing Room' held by Queen Victoria in 1877, but he may have developed a taste for the thrills of the courtroom, because the legal process became an important feature of his life.

It started off innocently enough. He was the victim of a burglary when his bag was stolen from a house belonging to a Mrs Allen. The burglar was discovered hiding under a table by a maidservant, Elizabeth McFarlane. The maid was clearly no coward. *The Times* reported that she knocked down the 20-year-old burglar and, when he got up and attacked her with a candlestick, she held on to him until help came. The burglar got 12 months hard labour, and the Judge recommended that Elizabeth should get a reward. Berney, interviewed by *The Times*, said that she was 'a respectable girl'. It's rather reassuring to know that he recognised one!

Berney was a regular habitué of the courts. In 1862 he brought a case against Mr Wright, an employee of Messrs Pickford, alleging that the man had stolen some wine from two casks which had been consigned to him. Berney claimed that it was clear from scratches on the bung that it had been tampered with, but the cask remained full. When it was pointed out that he had not proved any loss, he claimed that the loss was not of quantity but of quality suggesting that it was quite possible for the man to have removed a gallon of wine and replaced it with a gallon of water. He claimed that the disappointing quality of the wine was because it had been so watered down. The Mayor, sitting on the bench, was irritated by Berney and said, effectually, that he could not use inference as evidence. Case dismissed, but not before the Bench suggested to Berney that he should seek professional advice before bringing other cases—advice that Berney clearly decided totally to ignore. As a postscript to this story the *Norfolk Chronicle* reported a couple of months later that Mr Wright had received a letter of apology from Berney and had so advised the Bench.

Having tried the role of advocate in the wine case, he next took on the role of policeman. In 1878 while driving in his carriage, Berney claimed to have heard an explosion of gunpowder and seen three boys who he chased. Having caught up with one of them he took him to the police station. In court, the exchange with the defence lawyer was vintage Berney:

Lawyer: What are you Mr Berney?

TB: *I am a clergyman.*

Lawyer: Are you a police officer duly appointed under the Police Act?

TB: *I decline to answer such a question.*

Lawyer: Are you a police officer appointed by the proper authority?

TB: *It is an absurd question.*

Lawyer: I must trouble you to answer it,

TB: *I am not a police officer.*

And on it went, Berney was asked if he had questioned the boy without warning him of his rights, why he hadn't simply reported the matter to the police and whether he could definitely identify that boy as the one with the explosives. The boy was discharged without delay. One senses that members of the Bench were all too familiar with Berney!

In August 1879 there came before the Court what the *Norfolk News* described as 'a very amusing case'. Reading the reports of the case it is difficult not to feel that all parties, apart from Berney as Plaintiff, at times had their tongues firmly in their cheeks. The case was brought by Berney against a spinster aged 92, Miss Smith, who was the owner of a farm at Bracon Ash. Berney claimed that her servants and agents had shot game on land that was his 'free warren', effectually property over which he had sole sporting rights. Those rights had come into his family in 1729 but they dated back to the year 1256. At this point the Judge, perhaps smothering a sigh, asked whether this matter had been before the courts before. Mr Day, QC, for Miss Smith replied that it had come up the year before and indeed at every Assize. 'I thought I remembered the case' replied the Judge.

There followed an introduction by Sir Patrick Colquhoun, QC, for Berney, whose stated intention of proving the existence of the manorial rights from the time of Henry ll drew from the Judge the question 'Is this necessary?'. Mr Day suggested that they started going back from 1829, the year in which a previous case had decided that the sporting rights no longer went with the title to the land. Despite Berney's counsel trying to cite cases dating back to the time of Henry VI the judge made it clear that the right of 'free warren' had been extinguished. Berney's counsel then argued that shooting rights were distinct from free warren and Berney went into the witness box. Under cross-examination it came out that he had twice visited Miss Smith, with a view to obtaining her signature to a document confirming that the shooting rights were his, again the exchange on cross-examination was vintage Berney:

Mr Day: Did you take any writing with you?

TB: No, but I took pen, ink and paper.

Mr Day: Can you explain why you did not take your solicitor?

TB: Because I had gone in the previous year, in exactly the same way, to prevent Miss Smith or her tenant from exercising any undue rights over my manor.

Mr Day: Did your solicitor tell you that you ought to be ashamed of yourself to ask the old lady to sign?

TB: He never made any such impertinent remark.

Mr Day: Did you consult him before you went?

TB: No, I wished to prevent a law suit.

Mr Day: I thoroughly understand your benevolent motives.

There was laughter in the court, but Mr Day went on to allege that Berney had shaken his fist at the lady who was lying on her death-bed. Berney didn't answer this directly but proceeded to tie himself in knots.

This was not the end of the matter. Five years later Berney was in court again about the same land, this time as the defendant. Miss Smith had died, and her farm had been purchased by Sir Kenneth Kemp, who was the plaintiff in the case, and Berney arranged for the road leading to the property to be locked and barred. It was said in court that the claimant knew Berney 'was a gentleman who had sustained many lawsuits arising from his claim as lord of the manor, concerning which he had very exalted views as to his rights and privileges', even if 'he had not, hitherto, been fortunate in enforcing them in a court of justice'.

Not only had Berney installed locked gates but he had employed men to keep a 24 hour watch on them. On one occasion he went himself at 4 a.m. to check and finding the duty guard had failed to turn up sacked him. The Judge made what he described as the offer of an olive branch, trying to encourage Berney to acknowledge the plaintiff's rights, so as to stop the case, but Berney blundered on, telling counsel for the plaintiff (with, reported the press, an impatient gesture) not to interrupt him. There followed one of the best put-downs of the many Berney received from any number of Benches 'You may say what you like when you are in your proper place, the pulpit, but when you are in a court of justice you must conform to the rules of the court'. Giving judgement his lordship described the case as 'the most indefensible action ever brought to court, granted the injunction and awarded the plaintiff exemplary damages, saying that he saw no reason to reduce them by 'taking off the smallest coin of the realm' given the way Mr Berney had been trying to conduct his case. 'Oh, stuff!' responded Mr Berney.

In later life Berney applied himself to writing tracts and pamphlets on religious matters such as the snappily entitled:

'Marriage with a deceased wife's sister or with a niece contrary to the Holy Law of God and customs of the Jews, to the teaching of Our Lord Jesus Christ, and of his Apostles, and of Nature', which was published in 1885.

In 1882 he had written an open letter to Gladstone, gratuitously copied to 'Every member of the legislature' running to about 5000 words. It was a strong condemnation of the plans for a possible Channel Tunnel the existence of which, he feared, could result in an invasion by the French army. In enormous detail he described how an invading army, by tying strings to the triggers of their rifles could shoot the defenders of Dover Castle without emerging from cover themselves before taking the castle. In breathless prose he described how the telegraph wires could be taken over by holding a pistol to the head of the telegraph boy, thus cutting off in mid-message the telegram sent by a siege survivor to the War Office. He visualised a train with a battalion of Guards sent to stem the invasion being destroyed by a shell 'striking the periphery and flange of the great driving wheel of the locomotive... breaking the two after wheels to fragments'. He had calculated that it would take a '400lbs, 10-inch projectile with a maximum velocity of 1364 feet per second and an energy equal to 5562 tons' to do the task. He even drew a plan showing how this would happen. He went on to describe how the Officers would be flung off the train before being hit by the tender which would 'turn up in the air', and 'making a complete somersault', before landing on them. He didn't offer any explanation as to the required accuracy of the shot. This was followed by a graphic description of the scene in similarly robust and extravagant language. He asked Gladstone to lay copies before Queen Victoria, The Prince of Wales and the Duke of Cambridge, as Commander in Chief. One doubts he did, or that he got much further than the first couple of lines.

No-one could accuse Berney of lacking imagination, but he was certainly extraordinarily arrogant and very eccentric. Perhaps the most charitable interpretation one can put on his letter to Gladstone, as on his life, is that he had more loose screws than a flat pack furniture kit.

He continued in post as Rector, single, and living in Bracon Hall until his death in 1895. And the Cummings? The Revd Cumming remained Rector of East Carleton until 1907. A Rectory was provided in East Carleton itself in the early 1870s. As for Bessie, it seems that her experiences with Thomas Berney didn't put her off the clerical profession. She married an Oxfordshire parson.

> *The School accounts are 'illegal, informal and unintelligible and should be disembowelled'.*

The opinion of two of the Governors of the Norfolk County School 1876.

The Revd J L Brereton

Parish Priest, Educational Reformer & Founder of the Norfolk County School, Agriculturalist, and Railway Enthusiast

The sixteenth of September 1874 was a day of continuous rain—hardly auspicious weather for the official opening of the Norfolk County School near North Elmham. Perhaps the rain contributed to the unexpected absence from the ceremony of two of its most distinguished supporters, the Lord Lieutenant, Lord Leicester, and the Bishop of Norwich. Despite their absence about 180 invited guests, including the Earl Fortescue and Lord Sondes, sat down to lunch to celebrate the achievement of The Revd Prebendary Joseph Brereton, whose brainchild the school had been. The lunch was long, the speeches even longer. One of the guests (the great grandfather of the author) recorded in his diary 'there was much speaking, but it was indifferent in character'. It might have been the rain, it might have been the indifferent speaking, but the proceedings were so lengthy that by the time that the health of the school's architect, Mr Giles, was proposed it was discovered that he had left and gone to catch his train home.

The Revd Joseph Lloyd Brereton, who had already founded a successful County school in his previous Devon parish, was a quite remarkable man who succeeded his father, Charles, as Rector of Little Massingham in 1867. Brereton (senior) had married a Miss Frances Wilson, daughter of a wealthy silk magnate who, as was then the way, ramped up his social position by buying an estate. Declining to bid for Sandringham, which was on the market at the time, he bought at Little Massingham an estate of more than 2000 acres, a property which included the Rectory and gave him the right, as patron, to nominate a new Rector when the post became vacant.

Fortunately for Charles, just a year after his 1819 marriage, the previous Rector died, and the living became available for him to be instituted there. He remained as Rector for 47 years until shortly before his death. His marriage to Miss Wilson was blessed with eleven children several of whom made a substantial mark, but it is Joseph, who was born in 1822, who did so in the field of education.

Charles was a man of social conscience, and author of several pamphlets on subjects ranging from the operation of the poor laws to the role of rural police. He held a somewhat idealistic view of rural life, with the community 'managed' by the parson and the squire in a harmonious and paternalistic partnership.

Sometimes such partnerships worked, sometimes they foundered because of divergent views or personalities. The classic example was at Ketteringham where the squire, Sir John Boileau, fought a long war of attrition with what he described as 'his' parson, The Revd Andrew. This saga was the subject of Owen Chadwick's book *Victorian Miniature*, and became both bitter and personal. But that famous case was not unique. At Bradenham, the somewhat volcanic Squire Haggard (father of Rider Haggard) was continually at odds with The Revd Stone, an eccentric Irish clergyman. Stone once entered the village school where, without seeking parental consent, he proceeded to cut the hair of some of the children, causing great resentment amongst the parents. A man with a fuse as short of that of his Squire, on another occasion Stone threw his books onto the floor and stomped out of the school in anger. My great grandfather, the vicar of neighbouring East Dereham, was the unwilling recipient of the confidences of both his friend, Haggard, and his eccentric neighbouring cleric, recording in his diary that 'I'm afraid they will never get on'. Stone, soon after the haircutting incident, returned to Ireland.

Such shindigs were not an issue for Charles Brereton and his father-in-law. Charles' benign and caring approach may have been an early influence on his son, but it seems generally accepted that the inspiration behind Joseph's lifelong commitment to the cause of educational reform was Thomas Arnold, his Headmaster at Rugby, which he attended for three years from 1838. Certainly, in later life he said that his 'reverence and affection' for Dr Arnold had been a major influence on his life.

Prior to his time at Rugby his education had been partly at home, and then as a day boy at Islington Proprietary School, an experience which may have been another influence on the nature of the educational reforms for which he was later to become noted. His late entry to the more robust life of a nineteenth century boarding school was probably due to concerns about his health. Examination of the Baptismal records for Little Massingham shows that Joseph was baptised far sooner after his birth than most of his siblings. Early Baptism was often a sign of concern as to the infant's health.

His subsequent time at Oxford was punctuated by periods of absence due to illness. He had gone up on a Scholarship to University College and graduated BA in 1847, the year of his ordination. His results were not apparently as good as anticipated—a situation ascribed to his chronic health issues. Despite these difficulties he distinguished himself by winning, in 1844, the Newdigate Prize for poetry, a distinction which had been won the previous year by Matthew Arnold, son of his Rugby Headmaster, and which was later to be won by both Oscar Wilde and John Buchan.

It was during a leave of absence from Oxford on health grounds in 1844 that Brereton first experienced education from the other perspective, as a provider; he became private tutor to an Oxford student resident in Cornwall, an early introduction to the West Country where he was to spend more than fifteen very productive years before returning to Norfolk shortly before the death of his father. The student was the nephew of a member of an old and distinguished West Country family, the Pole-Carews.

Later, after completing his degree, Brereton was ordained in Norwich Cathedral and became, briefly, curate of St Edmunds, Norwich, before taking up another curacy in London at St Martins in the Fields. But the attractions of either the West Country or involvement with education, or perhaps both, must have been strong because in 1850 he went to live near Torquay with the aunt of his former student. He had no clerical appointment to take up, rather he moved with a view to setting up as a private tutor. While there he met and married, in 1832, Frances Martin, the daughter of a deceased local parson—they were to have sixteen children, of whom no less than five (of the eleven who survived to adulthood) were to become priests. Three of his own sons followed their grandfather and father successively as Rectors of Little Massingham. Altogether these five family members were the incumbents for a continuous period of a hundred and twenty-one years, from 1821 to 1942. Such were the joys of family patronage.

Soon after his marriage Brereton accepted the living of West Buckland, in Devon, where he was to remain happily for fifteen years, an incumbency marked by his most enduring achievement, the foundation of the Devon County School, now West Buckland School.

While in the West Country, Brereton was to prove a significant force not just in educational reform, but also in the development of railways and the advancement of the agricultural interest. Of the three, the cause of educational reform was perhaps the most important to him and before looking at his achievements it is worth examining the factors that may have influenced his beliefs. Reference has already been made to the influence of Dr Arnold, but there is a strong case to be made for Brereton having been influenced by his pre-Rugby experience, too.

His first experience of formal education had been at Islington Proprietary School. Note the word 'proprietary' because the belief in schools funded by proprietors was at the heart of Brereton's vision. His ambition was to create affordable private education under a broad religious umbrella for the sons of middle-class parents in schools controlled not by the state or the Church, but by their proprietors. These were to offer boarding, especially for those such as the sons of farmers who might be disadvantaged by living too far from large centres of population to attend strong academic day schools, and by the inadequacy of their parents' income to pay the fees of the major Public Schools.

Islington, where he went as a day boy, had been established in 1830. At the time of its establishment its rules and aims were embodied in a single document, which stated that while it was to be founded 'upon the principles of the Church of England, the religious instruction will be so conducted as to embrace the children of all who wish for an education on the basis of the great doctrines of Christianity'.

Rule 1 (of 48) set out the purpose of the school:

> The object of the Institution is to provide a course of Education for youth, to comprise classical learning, the modern languages, mathematics, and such other branches of useful knowledge as may be advantageously introduced; together with religious and moral instruction, in conformity with the doctrines and disciplines of the Church of England.

These words encompass Brereton's own later ambitions—to establish a type of education which was, literally, broad church, and which would provide a 'useful' education and not be simply restricted to the classics, within a fundamentally Christian environment. Indeed, in speaking at a celebration of its 25th anniversary at the Devon County School his speech specifically referred to the inclusion of Nonconformists within that broad-church concept and stressed again the need for the secular part of the curriculum to educate pupils so as to satisfy the requirements of both public and private enterprise. At a time when the Anglican Church was riven with schism between 'High' and 'Low' and fighting a rearguard action against the advance of Methodism and the challenge of Darwinism this was a quite remarkably emollient and reasonable approach. It contrasted with the views of Nathaniel Woodard, the other great nineteenth century clerical founder of schools for the middle classes, who would have no truck with nonconformists and little with low church Anglicans.

The detail of the technical aspects of Islington's rules, set out later in the founding document, clearly influenced Brereton's own later plans. There was to be a minimum of 100 proprietors, subscribing £15 each, with no subscriber being able to hold more than two shares. Fees for pupils were to be limited to an annual payment of ten guineas (£10.50 in modern parlance) a fraction of the fees charged at traditional public schools. The Proprietors had rights and obligations, effectually managing the school with the appointed Head who, in Brereton's time there, was John Jackson, a future Bishop of London.

Later, as the incumbent of a rural parish at West Buckland, Brereton's understanding of the limitations on the type of education available to the children of his farming parishioners was reinforced. Farming was another of his interests—while there he founded the Barnstaple Farmers Club.

Some sources suggest that this was as early as 1854, but the *Western Times*, reporting in September 1866 on the opening of a new hall for the club, suggests that it was as late as 1865, shortly before Brereton's return to Norfolk. The Club, having been founded 'to promote intercourse amongst the agriculturalists of the neighbourhood', appointed Brereton as President. At the dinner celebrating the club's new premises Brereton declared that 'Agriculture was not the sister but the mother of all peaceful enterprise'. Whichever is the true date of foundation Brereton was undoubtedly an enthusiastic agriculturalist and laboured hard for the provision of compensation for farmers facing natural disaster, not always successfully. A campaign he led in 1866 to raise a rate to compensate farmers for losses as a result of the 'cattle plague' foundered for lack of non-agricultural support. The people of Crediton, for example, were, he was advised, so strongly adverse to the plan that 'there was no point in proposing such a resolution as there was not a shadow of a chance of carrying it'.

Brereton stayed sufficiently interested in the success of the club to remain its President after he moved back to Norfolk. As President he chaired the Annual General Meeting five years after he had left the county, in 1872, sitting, perhaps impatiently, through a lengthy debate about the club's liability to pay an overdue annual subscription of two guineas to the Devon County Chamber of Agriculture. Probably of more concern to him would have been the disclosure that the club's financial position was such that it had been unable to pay the honorarium due to the club secretary. Lack of finance, and perhaps lack of effective financial planning, were to play a significant part in the various enterprises espoused by Brereton over the years.

His foundation of the County School in Devon was made possible by Brereton's remarkable facility for attracting the rich and famous to his support. A member of an old and distinguished family himself, he soon found his way into the circle of the great and good of the county, perhaps assisted by the patronage of the aunt of his former pupil from his Oxford days. His most significant ally, and a lifelong friend, was Viscount Ebrington, later the 3rd Earl Fortescue. He and his father, the 2nd Earl, were enthusiastic supporters of Brereton's plans, perhaps contributing to their formation, and certainly to their execution. The 2nd Earl was also Lord Lieutenant of Devon and the owner of a large estate, opening what was to become the Devon County School in 1858. The 3rd

Earl was also involved with Brereton in the pursuit of his other passion, the development of the railway; jointly they were involved in the development of the Taunton to Barnstaple line which subsequently became part of the Great Western Railway. Brereton's younger brother, Robert Maitland Brereton, had worked with Brunel in the development of the GWR before becoming a railway engineer both in India and the USA.

The Norfolk County School opened with high hopes and perhaps unrealistic expectations. The Foundation Stone was laid in April 1873 by the Prince of Wales, who donated £250 to establish

Laying of the foundation stone of the Norwich County School, Easter Monday, 1873.

a scholarship in his name. The site was donated by Lord Leicester, who also subscribed £1000 of the initial £10,000 capital raised to establish the school. Some of the contributors were from 'County families' but with shares pitched at £10 there were plenty of takers from the farming community also. Brereton calculated that 200 boarders paying fees of just over £40 p.a. each would provide an adequate income to run the school effectively, while allowing a reasonable return to the shareholders. In what was effectively a prospectus for his 'County' schools, Brereton aimed to attract investors who would receive a dividend of not more than 5% to provide the finance. As the rate on Consols at the time was 3% (and later fell) the extra potential 2% may have seemed a reasonable risk premium to some.

Ambitious and optimistic, Brereton set out to provide accommodation not for 200 boarders but for 300—he had started with just seven pupils when he had opened a small school at Great Massingham in 1871 in an old house, formerly the home of a local doctor. Two of the pupils were his own sons. In the school magazine of 1878 a pupil describes how, as numbers grew to thirty, the school first moved to Little Massingham Rectory and then all thirty moved on to North Elmham together when it opened. Perhaps Brereton's expectations had been optimistic in Massingham too—the *Norfolk News* of 18 July 1874 included an advertisement to sell items which would be surplus to requirements after the move to North Elmham. Amongst the items to be sold were 60 beds and 250 plates, for 30 pupils! The plans for the new school were drawn up by the architects John Giles & Gough, who were later to design Cavendish College, Cambridge, another of Brereton's projects. The contract to build the property, at a cost of £8000, was given to a Dereham based builder and, was, remarkably, completed in time for that official opening in the rain of September the following year.

The plans were on a grand scale. At the opening the

The Norfolk County School.

reporter from a local paper waxed lyrical in the prolix fashion of the day—'one is reminded at once of days long ago and of the palaces in which the princes of the land were prone to dwell'. Certainly, the premises were palatial, the main hall was eighty feet long, forty wide, and fifty high, and the exterior of flint dressed with red brick was imposing, with large dormers and turrets. Development continued after the opening with a chapel, a swimming pool and boathouse added.

The Director's Report for 1874 was broadly optimistic but disclosed that the anticipated total costs of establishing the school were now £16,000 or 60% more than the original £10,000 raised and that their calculations were based on 260/270 boarders. They warned that shareholders should be prepared for 'lingering and fluctuating progress' towards these numbers.

But even the originally anticipated 200 boarders needed to make the school viable never materialised. Seventy were admitted originally, and this grew to over 100 by 1881. Apart from the disappointing numbers, and the fact that many of the pupils were not the expected sons of local farmers, the school was successful. Examination results were good and past pupils went on to distinguish themselves in various fields. At an early Prize Day, the student in first place was presented with the poems of Macaulay and the second a Life of Wellington. It would be pleasing to detect a note of irony in the choice of the Prize awarded to the relative laggard who came third— a copy of Samuels Smiles' Self-Help! Probably the happiest prize winner was the boy who won a copy of Walton's Compleat Angler—the school had bought the fishing rights along with the freehold of the property.

The School ran into financial problems quite early. In

March 1876 Brereton presided over an uncomfortable special shareholders meeting, called because a previous meeting had not been quorate. The issue was the school accounts which two of the directors declared to be 'illegal, informal and unintelligible' and which one of them said in a letter read out loud at the special meeting should be 'disembowelled'. Given the language it is not surprising that feelings ran high. The report of the meeting in the Norwich Mercury of 1st April that year makes extraordinary reading. The accounts were referred to Messrs Price, Waterhouse and Co who concluded that, while they did not conform in every particular to the legal requirements, the firm had no reason to suppose that they were not an accurate reflection of the school's financial position. Reading between the lines of the press report, four things are evident. First, that the finances were not managed as effectively as they should have been, and that Brereton was more a big picture man rather than an analyst of detail. It may have touched a nerve that it came out that he owed the school over £800. His naivety was Brobdingnagian in scope; he described how, at a meeting held to discuss the establishment of the school he had agreed to subscribe for twice as many shares as he had planned to before the meeting, on a whim, while never 'thinking it right that he should incur any expense with regard to the school'. Second, that he saw the comments of the two dissenting directors as a very personal insult— rarely can umbrage have been more obviously taken. Third, it was clear that the shareholders present were entirely supportive of all the work Brereton had done in developing the school. Fourth, that the attendance of Mr Birkbeck, a partner in Gurney's Bank, must have been both a considerable calming influence on any nervous shareholder, and a restraint on those shareholders pressing for the meeting to pass a motion to pay a dividend. The irony is that, having begun the meeting clearly distressed by what he interpreted as a personal attack, and having defended himself at some length, even by reference to the Book of Psalms, Brereton finished the meeting with the support of those attending ringing in his ears and with a motion passed writing off his debt to the school.

Sadly, 1881 was the high point, numbers began to fall rapidly and the financial position of the school became unsustainable. By 1891 there were just sixteen pupils. The decline in numbers came at a time when Brereton was unable to contribute as industriously as he always had before. On 28 July 1882 he was travelling with his brother, General John Alfred Brereton of the Bengal Infantry, on a Great Eastern train from Cambridge to King's Lynn when, just south of Ely, while travelling at about 50 mph there was a collision with a piece of a train travelling in the opposite direction which, having been inadequately secured, became dislodged. As a result, both he and the General had been severely injured. He took the railway company to court, giving evidence that the severity of the impact had caused him to lose consciousness. After an hour lying by the side of the railway he had been taken by another train to Cambridge where he was kept in hospital until September and had subsequently been treated in London. Although he had tried to resume his parochial duties, he had found this impossible in the winter and had been obliged to employ a curate but could, by the date of the case (1884), manage to dispense with crutches and walk with just sticks. He estimated his financial loss at £450. His friend Earl Fortescue gave evidence of Brereton's 'remarkable mental power' and the Cambridge doctor attested that it was unlikely that he would ever recover full use of his leg or 'ever regain his mental vigour'. The case was proved and Brereton was awarded the sum of £4,000 (something like £400,000 today) in damages, his brother the General was awarded £6,500. By this time Brereton was deeply involved with another of his projects, Cavendish College in Cambridge, so how much energy and effort he might have been able to bring to the problems of the County School had he not been injured is questionable, but the accident cannot have helped.

The later days of the school were clearly sad for all involved. The *Norfolk News* reported the proceedings of a dinner held for the old boys in April 1893. The Chairman in proposing the health of both the school and the Headmaster acknowledged the school 'had, for some time, been in a very unsatisfactory state' and appealed to the former pupils to 'induce their friends to send their children to the school '(Loud Cheers, reported the press). The Headmaster, Mr Humphreys, replying to the Toast said that the reasons for the state of the school were not hard to find. The agricultural depression had been worse in East Anglia than elsewhere. This meant that farmers who would otherwise have sent their sons were resorting instead to Board Schools. He admitted that the numbers of pupils had been steadily declining and, echoing the Chairman, suggested that the remedy lay in the hands of the old boys to find additional pupils. This time the press reported that there was loud applause rather than loud cheers and the speech was followed, perhaps a little inappropriately, by the rendition of two comic songs.

The efforts of the old boys were clearly not enough; by 1895 the school had closed, and the premises remained empty for several years. They were visited by Dr Barnado who was seeking additional locations for children's homes and in 1899 they were purchased for Barnado's by a benefactor, shipowner E H Watts. By 1903 the school was operating as the Watts Naval Training College and operated under the Barnado flag until final closure in 1953.

Brereton's later projects proved just as temporary. At the time of his railway accident he was heavily involved in the development of another of his visions—moving the affordable education of the middle class and farming communities into the tertiary sector. He had founded Cavendish College in Cambridge on the same 'proprietary' basis some years earlier, intending to use it as a connecting link between his 'County Schools' and full degrees. His plan was for admission as young as 15 with a view to working for a new kind of certificate to be called a 'County degree'. This would have had no status as a Cambridge degree but those who remained after completion of the new certificate could stay on and do a full degree. As with North Elmham his vision fell down on practicalities, particularly the lack of students in sufficient numbers to render his grandiose scheme viable. The college closed in 1892 and the building was later purchased by Homerton College, which moved there from the East End of London.

In 1880 he established an organisation called the Graduated County Schools Association which sought to develop a parallel set of schools to those at West Buckland, but for girls. Again, the plans were ambitious, no less than eight boarding schools were acquired before the project collapsed after just seven years, with questions as to the quality of its financial management.

The financial problems so many of Brereton's projects experienced did not arise from a failure to understand the need to plan. All of them had business plans and projections, all of which on the face of it made the schemes look viable, or at least sufficiently so to attract investors. But a business plan is only as good as its inputs and some of Brereton's inputs, especially about numbers of pupils, would have made Wilkins Micawber appear a rank pessimist. There are some signs that his colleagues, at least in one enterprise, began to realise his limitations. There is a suggestion, though I have found no corroborative evidence, in respect of Cavendish College, that towards the end attempts were made to exclude him from any involvement with the financial aspects of the college's management.

It is tempting to look back and try to assess the contribution made by figures from the past. Tempting, but difficult to evaluate what happened in the context of a different era. Much better to assess it by reference to the contemporary view of an individual, preferably by means other than the borderline-obsequious obituaries which were the Victorian norm. In the case of Brereton, I would cite two pieces of evidence. At the school prize day at West Buckland in 1874, the main speaker was the then Chancellor of the Exchequer, Sir Stafford Northcote. Northcote was the local Member of Parliament and aware of what Brereton had achieved. In his speech he compared Brereton's contribution to the country to that of Wolsey, describing Brereton as the man posterity would recognize as the one who had done most to win 'the great battle for the provision of middle-class education'. In fact, posterity has not remembered Brereton as much as it perhaps should have done but the sentiment was clearly meant.

The second also offers a clue not just to the general regard in which Brereton was held but also as to part of the reason for the relative failure of some of his later projects. In 1882 an appeal was made to raise funds for a testimonial to Brereton. In a file at the Norfolk Record

Office is a copy of the circular issued, and a handwritten list of some of the subscribers, including the Prince of Wales, Lord Hastings and the Gurneys. There is a host of letters commending his work, and a short list of those who had not replied. There is but one letter of refusal, from Mr Lee Warner of Walsingham. Lee Warner regretted his inability to contribute but explained that the diminution of income from his agricultural interests as the depression deepened meant that he felt obliged to cancel all such subscriptions.

It was unfortunate for Brereton that some of his more ambitious schemes coincided with a long and deep depression in the agricultural arena. He also made things difficult for himself. His belief that schools should be wholly independent of the state was not sustainable in the long term and his broad-church approach was not likely to appeal to either Anglican wing. Nonetheless he was able to persuade many influential and rich patrons to support his theories. Despite the failure of many of his projects he was clearly admired and loved. The comments by Northcote quoted above and the support for his testimonial in 1882 show that he was not just a man of vision but also of great charisma.

West Buckland School is a fine institution to have left as a memorial, but it is sad that the list of such memorials is not longer. Brereton may have been over ambitious and grossly over-optimistic, he may have had limited financial or business acumen but without doubt he was a man of energy, of charm and, above all, of vision. It would have been a privilege to have known him.

Canon Augustus Jessopp.

Dr Jessopp preached one of his eccentric
sermons without reference to the object
which had brought us together.

Diary entry of The Revd B J Armstrong, 2 September 1880.

Canon Augustus Jessopp

Headmaster, Parish Priest, Antiquarian and prolific Author.

Augustus Jessopp was born in December 1823, the youngest of ten children, into a comfortably off family. His father was variously a barrister, a tax inspector and an unsuccessful parliamentary candidate. He had an unsettled childhood, spent in a variety of places; although the family home was in Cheshunt, the Jessopps, like many contemporary English families of their class, lived on the continent for fairly lengthy periods. The reasons were usually financial, but that seems unlikely in this case, and his father still practiced in the English courts, even when the family lived in either Brussels or the Hague.

Jessopp's schooling began at a small preparatory school near Epping Forest whose advertisements in *The Times* bragged that the boys had separate beds! He went on briefly to a senior school in Stockwell before moving to another school in Germany. What all his schools seem to have had in common is that Jessopp didn't particularly like them and was unhappy at each. These experiences must have influenced him to set out to do things differently at the two schools of which he was later headmaster.

On leaving school, Jessopp's ambition of following his brother to Cambridge were initially ruled out by his father on financial grounds, and he was found a place in a shipping company in Liverpool, in which one of his brothers-in-law was a partner. Although it was only a couple of years before he was able to persuade his father to relent and allow him to go up to Cambridge, his stay in Liverpool was to prove a major factor in his future life. It was there that he met the daughter of the senior partner of the firm, Mary Anne Cotesworth, who was to become his wife.

From an early age Jessopp had literary interests and aspirations. An admirer of Coleridge from a young age his time at Cambridge reinforced and broadened his literary taste. He developed a great interest particularly in the work of John Donne. Indeed the first, some years later, of the many books he published was *Essays in Divinity by John Donne DD*, which he edited.

Graduating BA in April 1847 he was ordained Deacon just a month later and became curate of the parish of St Agnes, Papworth. He soon discovered that there was more to working in a country parish than simply preaching. He became the arbiter of village disputes and the 'first (and sometimes only) responder' in medical crises. The following year he married Mary Anne Cotesworth and together they became involved with education as providers for the first time in the village school founded by the Rector.

One of the attractions of a country living was that, despite the various expectations of his role, there was plenty of time to indulge his interest in writing and the research which preceded it. The downside was that, although he was still quite close to Cambridge, there was not immediately available to him the amount of material needed to feed his appetite to complete his work on Donne. After seven years he resigned his curacy and returned to live in Cambridge where he was not only able to access such material but also to find a publisher for his work. The book was published in 1855.

Despite some inherited wealth, life was not easy financially when he returned to Cambridge and he applied for various posts, initially with limited success but, after a year, and with his first work published, he was appointed as Headmaster of a school in Cornwall, Helston Grammar School. Teaching afforded, as with appointment to a country parish, at least during the holidays, the opportunity to indulge his taste for research. He found a school in decline, with very few pupils. Jessopp brought enthusiasm and energy to his role and was so successful that when, after three years, he applied for the Headmastership of Norwich Grammar School, he could point to how his stewardship at Helston had tripled the number of pupils.

His selection as Headmaster of Norwich came at a difficult time for that school. Established originally in 1096 it had received a Royal Charter in 1547, moving shortly afterwards to its current site, by the cathedral. Like Helston, the number of its pupils had waxed and waned, but hit a low of eight in the early 19th Century.

By the time of Jessopp's appointment it had recovered a little, with 30 pupils on the roll. The city of Norwich was just beginning to recover economically from a long decline and its renaissance was largely the result of the genius of a small group of predominantly Baptist and Methodist entrepreneurs. The traditional, classical, nature of the Norwich School's educational focus and its clear Anglican traditions did not have obvious appeal for the increasingly non-conformist professional classes who would have constituted its natural constituency.

Jessopp set out to change that, and his approach was

THE GRAMMAR SCHOOL

Norwich Grammar School.

symptomatic of the age. Thomas Arnold, at Rugby, had led the way. Although continuing, and valuing, the classical tradition Arnold had broadened the scope of the curriculum with the addition of subjects such as Mathematics and Modern Languages. He had changed the whole tenor of his school by the introduction of monitorial roles and by a focus on moral development. His practices were an influence on many other headmasters and Jessopp was no exception.

A broader curriculum was quickly introduced at Norwich and Jessopp went out of his way to align the ethos of the school more closely with that of the Public Schools which were increasing both in numbers and popularity. Unlike Arnold, he was also an enthusiast for organised team sport—his especial fondness was for cricket—and the time he had spent both at home and at school on the continent made him especially at ease with the introduction of French and German to the curriculum.

Jessopp introduced additional examinations and believed firmly in the motivational benefit of these and the resulting prizes and scholarships to encourage pupils to learn. As was generally the case, prizes comprised suitable books. In the library of Norwich School there is a copy of a book awarded to one pupil as a Divinity Prize in 1878. It was entitled *Norwich School Sermons*. Whose sermons? Why, Jessopp's of course!

There seems little doubt that the lack of encouragement he had experienced as a pupil himself made him determined to promote the development of enquiring minds in his pupils. He didn't simply confine himself to modernising the curriculum, but the buildings as well. The result of all these changes was not just an increase in numbers, the roll also showed a significant increase in the proportion of boarders. The school's reputation was spreading well beyond Norwich, and Jessopp's influence and actions earned praise from the Schools Inquiry Commission, which inspected the school in 1867. He responded to any implied criticism of the school firmly. As early as 1860 he engaged in a heated correspondence with a critic published in the Norfolk News, asserting that five sevenths of the boys in the three upper classes were destined for University admission. (*Norfolk News*, 23 June 1860).

Jessopp's methods both encouraged and rewarded serious study, and, in particular, private study, but he had created an environment which was far from being one of just dry as dust scholarship. Contemporary accounts suggest an atmosphere in which there was encouragement of individuality, a real degree of freedom and a strong level of mutual respect between pupils and Headmaster.

If there was a blot on the landscape as far as Jessopp was concerned, it was his variable relationship with the Governors. In 1867 he publicly criticised the Governors for deciding to increase the level of school fees and reduce the level of Exhibitions and prizes. Parts of the local press endorsed his criticism suggesting that the proposed changes were 'injurious to the school and distasteful to the citizens generally' (*Norfolk Chronicle*, 5 October 1867). The *Norwich Mercury* was more circumspect, implicitly criticising Jessopp for raising the issue before the Governors had arrived at a final decision. Presumably Jessopp had done so primarily in order to seek to influence that decision.

The Governors were in an unenviable position. The same foundation funded both Norwich Grammar School and the Norwich Commercial School, which had opened in 1862 with the intention of educating boys to work in the newly developing trades and industries as the city continued its economic recovery. Within five years the Commercial School had a roll twice that of Norwich School. More important locally, the number of dayboys was four times as great, yet the bulk of available funds was allocated to the Grammar School. In 1867 there was an unseemly public argument between Jessopp and his opposite number at the Commercial School carried out in the columns of the local press, and the matter rumbled on for years, though Jessopp succeeded in getting the Governors to drop the fee increase. By a combination of his press activity and his private conversation with Governors he demonstrated that he had both bark and bite.

The freedom to develop his literary career did not bring as much benefit as he might have hoped from his role as Headmaster. The job involved long hours, especially when running a boarding house, and Jessopp had also become heavily involved in many other activities in the city. It may be reasonable to infer that the limit his other responsibilities imposed on the time available to develop his literary interests was one of the reasons why, after twenty years, he resigned his Headmastership and opted to return to a country parish. He had achieved much and, despite the funding issues which still rumbled on, he left a school which was in a much healthier state than the one he found on appointment. His qualities as Headmaster were widely recognised and appreciated, even by the Governors with whom he had argued. He was invited to become a Governor himself, and later became their Chairman. In his biography of Jessopp, Norfolk's Antiquary, Nick Hartley tells us that a group of former pupils clubbed together to buy the furniture he needed for his new study in the Rectory.

The country parish to which he was instituted in 1879 was the village of Scarning, near East Dereham, whose Vicar at the time was the author's great grandfather who had already been in post for nearly 30 years.

Despite some early hesitation, Armstrong, having invited Jessopp to preach at Dereham had found the sermon extraordinary, very confused and 'not likely to do any good', Jessopp and his wife were amongst a very few guests invited to Dereham Vicarage for lunch with the Bishop only a few months after his arrival in Scarning. The men must have discovered quite a lot in common. Not only were they both Cambridge men but, in their youth, both had ridden to hounds and shot. Their respective fathers were both Justices of the Peace and Deputy Lieutenants—Jessopp for Essex, Armstrong for Middlesex. Both fathers were, for the most part, comfortably off but each also had a daughter whose marriage demanded ongoing financial support, and each of them had also provided some financial support for their sons. Both sons had been influenced by the Oxford Movement when at University, Armstrong considerably more than Jessopp. They shared too a somewhat sceptical view of the Temperance Movement. Jessopp feeling that he could not do without the occasional glass of wine and that the working man should not be deprived of his glass of beer, while Armstrong argued that, for the working man, going to the pub served the same benefit as gentlemen got from going to the club. With so much in common it is not surprising that Armstrong welcomed Jessopp's arrival in Scarning as a neighbouring clergyman. They knew each other already, having met soon after Jessopp's arrival in Norwich, in 1859 Armstrong's diary refers to attending 'a gentleman's party' at Tuddenham Rectory in October 1860 at which Jessopp was a fellow guest, but the latter's arrival at Scarning was seen by Armstrong as a valuable addition to his range of local clerical acquaintance, affording the opportunity for more academic and stimulating conversation than was generally available. They became regular dinner guests at each other's homes, Armstrong averring that there was always 'interesting conversation' when they dined together.

But Jessopp's move to Scarning was not without its problems for him. Attitudes had changed since he had last worked in a country parish a quarter of a century earlier. The Revd Cubitt, his predecessor, who had recently died, had boots which should not have been too difficult to fill if my great grandfather's assessment was correct. In his diary on 1st August 1879 Armstrong wrote of Cubitt's incumbency

> I fear he has not done much good as he never seemed to have a sense of the office of a priest. Whisky at the hotel at 11.00 a.m., and pipe smoking in a town like this are not practices

which are calculated to raise the Church in people's minds.

Armstrong wasted no time in approaching Mr Evans Lombe, the patron of the living, and suggesting that his eldest son would be a suitable replacement! To no avail. Jessopp was selected but despite the perceived failings of his predecessor, he was not an immediate success at Scarning.

Perhaps the average villager was less deferential than a generation earlier. Perhaps Jessopp had, during his last Headmastership, acquired a somewhat superior air about him. Perhaps the worsening Agricultural Depression prejudiced people against the clergy as part of the 'establishment'. Whatever the cause, Jessopp was received in Scarning with less than total enthusiasm.

Such unpopularity was probably unfair. Jessopp was genuinely concerned for the welfare of the country labourers whose wages were falling in the depression and whose housing was woeful.

Unfortunately, he found himself even more unpopular when he became involved in a dispute about the village school of which he was a Governor. It was almost a case of blaming the messenger for the message. In brief, a proposal from the Charity Commissioners (Scarning school had the benefit of a substantial endowment) to introduce a charge of one penny a week per child, thus freeing funds for other purposes, was accepted by Jessopp and the Governors. But it caused outrage amongst the parents who vented their spleen on Jessopp—even to the point, reportedly, of stoning his Rectory. Angry meetings were held in the village and Jessopp was the target of much abuse. The villagers then decided to establish a rival school, despite Jessopp's warnings that this was a mistake. He was right, soon the rival establishment closed, and the rebels returned to the original school, paying the required penny a week. Gradually the bitterness died down, and Jessopp became a much appreciated pastor.

Scarning did moreover free Jessopp, as he had hoped, to follow his interest in research and writing. His most prolific period dates from that time, although he had frequently been published in journals before then. In almost every year for nearly thirty years he had one or more works published. Much of his output was in the form of essays commenting on what he saw as the vagaries of village life or the role, and trials, of a rural parson. These essays were then gathered together and published in book form. With his first work, on Donne, Jessopp had struggled to find a publisher—his burgeoning reputation meant that this was no longer the case.

In the Norfolk Record Office is a letter to Jessopp from James Nisbet & Company, making him an offer, which to an author of today, would sound extraordinarily generous. 20% royalties, falling to 10% in respect of books sold at less than half price, a £50 advance (about £5000 in today's values) and a 50/50 split of profits on sales in the United States. But Jessopp doesn't seem to have tied the knot with Nisbet, perhaps he thought their telegraphic address—DIDACTIC—was a little too close to home. His principal publisher was T Fisher Unwin. He was in good company, at various times Unwin also published such authors as Somerset Maugham and John Galsworthy. Jessopp also wrote numerous pieces for magazines such as *The Illustrated London News* and *The Nineteenth Century*. All these published works helped to boost his income, as did the bequest received by Mary Anne from the estate of her father, who died shortly after the move to Scarning.

But Jessopp was much more than just a parish priest and prolific essay writer. He was a serious researcher with a deep interest in historical subjects, widely recognised for his knowledge. He was a member of the Norfolk and Norwich Archaeological Society of which he became Vice President, lecturing at their meetings and arranging some of their exhibitions. One academic with whom Jessopp forged a close friendship was M R James, then Dean of King's College, Cambridge. James was aware of Jessopp's skills and approached him to collaborate with James in translating from the Latin a series of manuscripts including one about St William of Norwich. M R James is perhaps today remembered best for his evocative ghost stories, which certainly scared me when my mischievous elder brother insisted on reading them to me when I was a small boy.

Jessopp also occasionally wrote about the supernatural.

Mannington Hall.

Augustus Jessopp claimed he saw an apparition in the Library in 1879.

He claimed personally to have experienced a phenomenon when staying at Mannington Hall in 1879. Sitting late at night in the Library at the Hall, examining and taking notes on various ancient documents, he claimed suddenly to have seen an ecclesiastically dressed figure of a man examining the books on which Jessopp had been working. The figure disappeared only when Jessopp a few minutes later reached out and picked up one of the books, subsequently reappearing only to disappear again when Jessopp threw down the book he was reading. At the time several explanations were offered, including the possibility that Jessopp had dozed off and was dimly aware of a figure when the manservant of his host crept into the room to take advantage of his doze by helping himself to a night cap! Jessopp wrote up the story and the press picked it up so that the tale became widely known. Locally it became the subject of dinner party conversation, according to Armstrong's diary, but the story was far more widely known than that.

Clearly Jessopp was an erudite man, a noted antiquarian and a gifted writer, and not without humour. He became sufficiently well known to be on friendly terms with some of the most significant literary figures of his day. But he was also a parish priest and in that aspect of his career he perhaps did not receive the preferment he felt his due. Such was the view of the writer of his obituary in the Eastern Daily Press of 14 February 1914, writing 'Men with not half his power and with far lower qualities of mind have, by virtue of the pushfulness (sic) which he lacked attained higher places in the Church……..Dr Jessopp was aware of that, and we believe felt, in connexion with Church affairs, something of the pain of neglect'.

The lack of 'pushfulness' is not, I feel, a wholly merited

observation. When writing about such an exemplary character as Augustus Jessopp it's always rather refreshing to find at least a little sign of human weakness. In Jessopp's case I came across something entirely by chance. When doing some research at the Norfolk Record Office in relation to another character in this book, I was going through a collection of the correspondence of Lord Walsingham when I spotted a letter written to him from Scarning Rectory. Reading it was enough to make me search for any further letters and I quickly found that in the course of just a few days Jessopp had showered his Lordship with no less than four. Jessopp clearly had a good intelligence network. He had learned 'on what ought to be good authority' that the current Dean of Norwich, Dr Goulburn, was planning to retire on health grounds, and Jessopp coveted the role. Like Jessopp, Goulburn had at one time been a Headmaster, in his case at Rugby. Jessopp first wrote to Lord Walsingham to solicit his support on 22 February 1889.

Perhaps disingenuously, Jessopp wrote that he was 'unskilled in applying for preferment', 'quite ignorant in how to set to work' and 'not at all sure that I am not venturing on an improper course in writing to your Lordship on the subject'. He managed to include all three remarks in one sentence. He then went on, with no sign of false modesty, to assert that 'the fact however is notorious enough, that there is a large number of people in the County of Norfolk who think—rightly or wrongly—that I have, during the last 25 years deserved well of East Anglia, to whom it would be a great pleasure to hear that I had been appointed as Dean Goulburn's successor'. No ambition for himself then, just happy to accept preferment to please others! He goes on to list his own qualities before repudiating these as a claim for promotion. 'A man's work is its own reward', he wrote, and went on to ask Lord Walsingham whether he would do him 'the great honour and great kindness to speak a word in my favour to Lord Salisbury'. In another burst of words showing no false modesty, he went on to list some of his more recent achievements, before winding up with a sentiment of which Uriah Heep might have been proud—'If in writing as I do, I am taking a step which is in your judgement unbecoming, I must plead my ignorance of what may be ye right course, and throw myself upon your charity to pardon an unintentional impertinence' signing himself off 'Your Lordship's obedient and humble servant'.

Jessopp wrote again on the 24th, concerned that his original approach might be seen as 'an indelicacy' and anxious because he had discovered that an approach had already been made to Salisbury on his behalf. The following day he wrote again, this time to say that he had discovered that his nephew had also written to Salisbury canvassing for his uncle's appointment and adding, somewhat unconvincingly, that he did not write to Walsingham 'as a petitioner in any sense'.

Walsingham must have replied promptly and in the affirmative, because Jessopp's next letter, on the 26th— three letters in as many days—was signed 'Your Lordship's obliged and humble servant', an impression confirmed by a letter from Salisbury to Walsingham saying that he would consider the recommendation but that there was, as yet, no vacancy, and when there was there would be a number of candidates.

Goulburn did retire, but Jessopp did not get the appointment. He may not have been too disappointed. His final letter to Walsingham, the one on the 26 February, disclosed that he had now discovered from his source (again 'on good authority') that the post was only worth £900 a year and 'such an income would clearly not be sufficient to keep up the ramshackle house and the inevitable expenses of such a position'. Perhaps it was a pity that his 'good authority' didn't tip him off originally about the level of stipend. It might have saved Lord Walsingham a fair amount of correspondence.

Any disappointment he may have felt at the lack of progress in his clerical career needs to be balanced against the reputational triumphs and significant financial rewards of his literary career, and the pleasure his writing and his company gave to those fortunate enough to know him. He was a remarkable man.

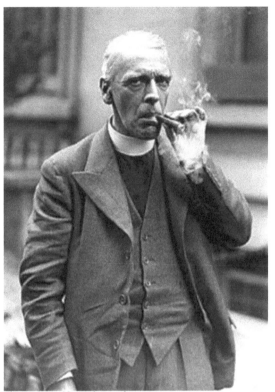

The Revd Harold Davidson on his way to court.

Very free with kisses—he kisses everybody!

Lady Weachter, a friend and supporter of The Revd Davidson, who helped to raise funds for his defence and stood with him as he left the court after his conviction (as quoted in defence councel's trial notebook).

The Revd Harold Davidson

the self-styled 'Prostitute's Padre', de-frocked for immoral behaviour on somewhat dubious evidence, and tragic victim of an angry lion.

At 10 o'clock on the morning of 29 March 1932, at Church House, Westminster, proceedings opened in the Norwich Consistory Court in one of the most extraordinary cases such a court had ever heard. The running of this particular hare had been started by Major Hamond, a distinguished and much decorated retired officer, who had been involved in a long running battle with Davidson on various matters and who became Churchwarden at Morston. His complaint to the Bishop of Norwich eventually led, after much hesitation and discussion, to the latter bringing a case against The Revd Harold Davidson, rector of Stiffkey and Morston, under the Clergy Discipline Act, 1892. The action comprised five charges, all relating to alleged immorality with young women. The defendant arrived to face his accusers smoking a large cigar and accompanied by his wife, to be greeted by a group of his supportive parishioners who had travelled down from North Norfolk to show solidarity with their extremely eccentric pastor.

Harold Davidson was certainly a very unconventional parish priest. Charged with the cure of souls in his remote Norfolk parish, he interpreted his mission as being to limit his parish duties largely to taking Sunday service, while spending the rest of the week in London rescuing young women whom he felt to be in moral danger, making their acquaintance by flattering them with compliments, such as effecting to mistake them for a famous film star, and then whisking them off to a local restaurant to learn their life stories. Sometimes it was the waitresses at the cafes that he engaged in conversation.

Apologists for Davidson, and there are a number, compare him to Gladstone. While it's true that both roamed the streets at night in search of 'fallen women' the similarity ends there. Gladstone took them back to Downing Street for a kitchen chat with himself and Mrs Gladstone. Davidson took them to restaurants, to the theatre, to Paris and, it was alleged, sometimes to bed as well. He certainly helped some of them financially. On the positive side he helped a number of them to find 'respectable' jobs and, like Gladstone, he did introduce some of them to his wife, though she was, to say the least, unamused to have them as house guests in the Rectory at Stiffkey; some complained that they were treated by her as skivvies. Two claimed actually to have been desperate enough to walk as far as Fakenham, sleeping in the fields, to find transport back to London. One photograph shows Mrs Davidson hiding behind a bush from a photographer at Stiffkey Rectory during a visit by two of her husband's protégées.

The case meant that Davidson's name was splashed on the front page of almost every paper. To such an extent was he the story that local daily papers up and down the country even reported the case when he was fined five shillings for riding his bicycle without lights! And he wasn't just famous for fifteen minutes; he managed to maintain a high profile right up until his death in

1937. From the start, his exploits were food and drink to the salacious, and the gruesome manner of his death, reminiscent of Stanley Holloway's monologue Albert and the Lion, ensured his continuing fame. The 1930s was a miserable decade; Davidson certainly enlivened it.

Harold Davidson was the son of a parson. Indeed he claimed that no less than 27 members of his family had been men of the cloth. His father, whose wife was an invalid, had a parish in a fairly seedy part of Southampton. At age 6, Harold was entered for a local private day school with a reputation for toughness, to which it lived up, and at 14 he moved on to Whitgift. He was neither the most reliable nor the most studious of pupils, disappointing his father's hope that he would win a University Scholarship to enable him to study for Holy Orders. Indeed, Harold's ambitions at the time lay more with the stage than the pulpit, and his first professional experiences were as an entertainer and as an actor in a touring repertory company though he remained an active Christian.

Later, thanks to the influence of a family friend, he was able to study for Holy Orders, originally at Exeter College, Oxford. It took him five years to complete a degree normally completed in three and by then Exeter had tired of him so he had enrolled at a crammer. Part of the reason for his slow progress was his need to earn enough, on the stage, to fund his studies. While still at Oxford he met an actress, Molly Cassandra Saurin, whom he married after an on/off six year engagement in 1906, the year he was appointed to the benefice of Stiffkey, whose patron was another eccentric, the 6th Marquess Townshend. Some thought that Davidson's appointment was a reward from Townshend for celebrating the latter's marriage— members of whose family had reputedly threatened to have him certified if it went ahead.

During the First World War, Davidson served as a naval chaplain and gave an early indication of things to come, he was arrested during a police raid on a Cairo brothel; his explanation was that he had visited the brothel to remonstrate with one of the girls who had infected a number of sailors with VD. Whilst he was away on war service, the youngest of the Davidson's five children was conceived. The disclosure of this during the trial greatly distressed Davidson who felt it damaging for the child, whom he treated as his own.

The trial was conducted by the Chancellor of the Consistory Court, Mr F Keppel North. One could infer from the transcript of the proceedings that not only was Mr North a little hard of hearing but also that he was out of the same mould as the lawyer who, in the Lady Chatterley obscenity case 30 years later, enquired of the jury whether it was the sort of book they would want their servants to read. Nor was his independence obvious. He was an old friend of the Bishop and apparently godfather to the Bishop's daughter. One can feel some sympathy for Mr North. The trial lasted 25 days—the closing address of Counsel for the Bishop lasted three of them. By that time evidence had been taken from 69 witnesses and the Chancellor's irritation with Davidson was, on occasion, evident. So much so that counsel appearing for Davidson even went so far in open court as to say to the Chancellor 'I should be glad if you would try to keep an open mind' an implied reprimand almost beyond belief from counsel in such circumstances.

Some of the evidence in the trial was sensational. The transcript is held at the County Record Office in Norwich; it fills four large boxes and is available for the public to read. The really enthusiastic can supplement this by reading it in conjunction with the seven large notebooks written throughout the trial by K J P Barraclough, one of the counsel for Davidson. Together, the two provide an astonishing record of an extraordinary trial. As interesting are the files of correspondence between the solicitors on either side; accusations are rife about potential witnesses being bribed, bullied and followed about by private detectives. The correspondence between the solicitors positively bristles with (carefully-worded) recriminations and threats. The case seemed to raise a tsunami of legal disagreements.

Not everyone will wish to sift through this mountain of paper to find the key statements; fortunately, they do not need to as two books on the case, *The Troublesome Priest* by Jonathan Tucker and *The Prostitute's Padre* by Hugh Cullen (both listed in the Bibliography), guide the reader through the main elements of the trial.

While there is no space, in just one chapter, to review the evidence in detail a little about some of it will give a flavour.

The first witness was Barbara Harris, who clearly enjoyed the momentary fame her appearance afforded her. Blonde, dressed to kill and wearing a succession of different hats, she arrived early to pose for press photographers. Quickly acknowledging that she was sexually experienced, had had intercourse with many men, both white and Indian, and had been treated for VD, she told the story of meeting Davidson. He had approached her at Marble Arch station when she was 16 years old, telling her she looked like a film actress and inviting her to visit a restaurant with him, an offer she accepted. When told of her (mainly financial) problems, Davidson had offered to help and turned up the next day at her lodgings, telling her landlady that he was her uncle. They knew each other for 18 months during which, she claimed, Davidson had made numerous unsuccessful attempts to seduce her, while paying her rent. She alleged that on one occasion he had attempted to rape her and then 'relieved himself' in front of her when she had succeeded in fending him off. It seems strange today that the language of such a witness was so oblique—presumably she had been coached in her choice of vocabulary. It is, perhaps, a commentary on the times that this coyness extended to Fleet Street whose editors appear to have ignored the kind of detail which would delight the modern 'red-top' press. This prissiness was seen elsewhere in the evidence when condoms, allegedly kept in Davidson's rooms, were described as 'preventatives'. Sometimes, Barbara claimed, he would take her to his own lodgings in Shepherd's Bush where she slept in the bed while he occupied a chair. When she went to live with an Indian policeman temporarily in London, Davidson visited them both, sipping tea while his hosts sat in bed in their pyjamas.

After the Indian went home Barbara moved into a separate room at Davidson's lodgings, where she alleged he continually made improper suggestions to her. She testified that he gradually moved from the chair, first onto and then into the bed with her, but that she continued to reject his advances. She never claimed that intercourse had taken place between them, but she had written a letter to the Bishop as proceedings started, in which she claimed that Davidson had 'the keys of a lot of girls' flats and front doors'. There is a rather charming innocence to some parts of Davidson's relationship with her. In one letter 'Uncle Harold' scolded her for some unkindness and enclosed a stamped addressed envelope for her to post him a letter of apology!

Another key witness might have been Rose Ellis, a girl he had met more than ten years before the case. He had helped her with money then and had found her work, even employed her briefly as a gardener at Stiffkey. She was one of those he had taken to Paris, with a view to finding her employment there. She was approached by detectives working for the prosecution and given clothes and money to encourage her to make a statement. When she agreed she was further encouraged by liberal measures of port to say her piece. Although the prosecutor referred to the relationship, Rose was not called as a witness, possibly because, when the effect of the port had worn off, she had second thoughts about her statement and claimed that the relationship was entirely innocent. Presumably the reason she was not called for the defence was that she had been served a subpoena by the prosecution.

Further evidence related to a third girl, Estelle Douglas, who was the daughter of an old friend of Davidson. The prosecution introduced a photograph of the 15 year old, wearing a shawl which was being held by Davidson. This was followed by a further picture, in which the shawl had 'slipped' revealing that Estelle was wearing nothing else. As with much other evidence in the case, caution needs to be exercised when considering these photographs. Clearly Davidson was very foolish to allow himself to be put in a position where such photographs could be taken, especially when he had already been charged, but it seems probable that he was set up. The photographs were taken at the flat of Estelle's mother (she was out) by two anonymous press photographers. Some 'saucy' poses were apparently suggested by the photographers but Davidson refused. He also claimed to have declined to

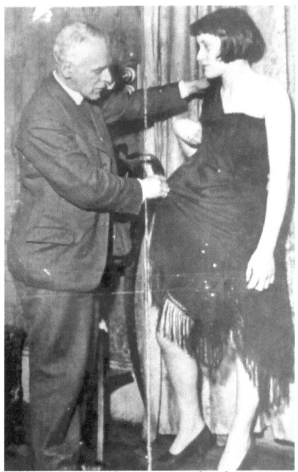

Photgraphic evidence presented in court against Revd Davidson.

accept a payment of £50 from one of the photographers
to pose for other pictures with Estelle, whose mother had
originally suggested the photo-session to promote Estelle's
modelling career. Estelle was to have been photographed
in a bathing costume, but the photographer persuaded
her that she should not wear one because the strap would
show. Davidson was to claim that he was totally unaware
of this at the time.

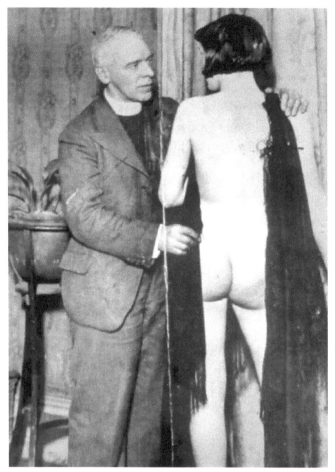

As with much else in the evidence, the incident bears hallmarks of a 'fix'. Quite apart from the surreptitious removal of the bathing costume there is doubt about how it was possible for the second picture to be taken. Davidson said he might have dropped the shawl when startled by the photographer's flashlight. Estelle, in evidence, suggested that either someone had pulled the shawl, or it had slipped just as the picture was being taken. Either way, Davidson seems to have been astonished by the revelation of Estelle's nakedness. In evidence Davidson claimed that the photographers had wanted to take the saucier shot because they could sell it to a Mr Searle. Searle was an employee of the firm of private detectives employed by the Bishop's solicitors to investigate the behaviour of Davidson. Indeed it was he who had plied Rose Ellis with port while interviewing her. Whether a fix or not the existence of the photograph was probably the final nail in Davidson's coffin.

The Court reconvened on 8 July for Chancellor Keppel North to deliver his judgement. As was frequently the case, proceedings started in Davidson's absence—that week he had been touring, appearing before sometimes disappointing audiences. *The Hartlepool North Daily Mail* had reported that Davidson had given a performance the previous night attracting an audience of just 200 in a hall which could accommodate 2000, and this in spite of being supported by 'a violinist, an entertainer and a vocalist'. By the time Davidson arrived he had already been found guilty on two counts, and more guilty verdicts followed. Chancellor North, perhaps a little bizarrely, as during her testimony she had admitted that 'she would do almost anything for money', appeared to swallow whole the evidence of such as Barbara Harris, who claimed to have continued her relationship with Davidson in spite of his alleged attempted rape of her, while dismissing Davidson as 'an awful liar', and his evidence as 'a tissue of falsehood'.

The Church proved unremitting in its harsh treatment of Davidson. Having been found guilty on five counts of immorality, there was a delay before sentence and the Bishop had not barred him from preaching. When he arrived at Morston Church to take a service he found it locked, and a sign outside that this was as 'a public protest' at his being allowed to continue preaching. The notice was signed by his old protagonist, Philip Hamond. The Bishop soon issued an 'inhibition' on Davidson continuing to preach, even though he had applied to appeal against the verdict. But one Sunday remained between the issuing of the inhibition and its coming into force, and Davidson preached to a huge congregation at Stiffkey before travelling on to Morston, where his attempt to discuss with Hamond the following week's service enraged the latter so much that he kicked Davidson on the bottom. As a local magistrate it must have embarrassed Hamond that he subsequently faced a charge of assault in a court where he normally sat on the Bench. He pleaded guilty and was fined £2.

Davidson's application to appeal was rejected and on 21 October 1932 he was subjected to the ordeal of sentence. The whole process seemed designed to humiliate him. The sentencing took place in Norwich Cathedral and was open to members of the public. The Bishop was accompanied by Chancellor North, the Dean, the Archdeacons and his legal advisers. They all had to wait, Harold Davidson had not arrived. He sent a cheerful and insouciant telegram to the Bishop explaining he might be a little late, but hoped there would be an opportunity to discuss parish business with the Bishop and the Archdeacon when the sentencing was complete. Eventually he arrived and, before the Bishop passed sentence, he made a statement reaffirming his innocence. The Bishop then proceeded formally to deprive Davidson of his living. It soon became clear that this was not to be the limit of his punishment. The Bishop, moving to the High Altar, continued by announcing that Davidson was 'to be entirely removed, deposed and degraded from the offices of priest and deacon'.

His disgrace was complete, not only was he to be deprived of his living at Stiffkey, but he was to be prevented from continuing in his profession at all. For a man who professed to believe that he was behaving to vulnerable and 'fallen' women in the way Christ would have done, and who believed that he was following a calling from God, this must have been extraordinarily painful. The sentence, and particularly the manner of its pronouncement, seem almost calculated cruelty.

Davidson appealed to the Archbishop of Canterbury but his application was turned down on 7 December 1932. He spent his few remaining years seeking a way to appeal against the verdict or raising funds to enable him to continue his fight. By the day of sentencing he was already actively seeking funds.

Given both his theatricality and his public persona it isn't surprising that Davidson's attempts to raise the necessary funds were in the full glare of publicity. Even before the sentence he had become a sideshow on the Golden Mile at Blackpool. Here he sat in a barrel, supposedly due to fast, though he denied this to the press, for a fortnight while holidaymakers paid two-pence each to see him. No ordinary barrel of course; it had a window so he could be seen and a chimney to clear his cigar smoke! His fee was to be £500 but the exhibition was short-lived. So popular was the novelty that thousands paid to see him (some reports suggested as many as 10,000 on the first day alone) and the local council took him and the showman behind the wheeze to court for 'obstruction'. The barrel-fasting was brought to an abrupt halt, though Davidson continued to parade in Blackpool, signing autographs while he continued to assert his innocence.

When it was clear no further right of appeal remained

open Davidson developed new tactics to promote his case, making statements about his accusers which seemed a quite deliberate attempt to provoke a response such as an action for defamation. Such a case would have afforded an opportunity to revisit the accusations, but if that was his intention it failed as the bait remained untouched.

Davidson's popularity began to diminish. His activities became more and more bizarre, and the authenticity of some of them was questioned. He even allowed himself to be exhibited with a mechanical imp spearing him in the posterior with a pitchfork.

His difficulties were not just a matter of his public image. He had long been pursued by his previous landlady for arrears of rent and, while he was in Blackpool, the bailiffs caught up with him. Having eluded them initially he later sought to escape them by shinning down a drainpipe but eventually gave himself up and served nine days in prison. The *Lancashire Evening Post* reported, in June 1933, that he had been injured while escaping down the drainpipe and was being treated at the hospital in Walton Gaol.

Undeterred he continued to seek opportunities to challenge the verdict of the court, and to raise the funds to do so. He also continued with his old habits, in 1936 approaching two teenage girls at Victoria Station and offering them £5 to audition for a new play. Reported by them to the authorities he was charged with 'trespassing on railway property', fined £7. 8s. 0d and ordered to pay up within 30 days or go to jail for 15. His failure to pay the fine gave rise to a rather entertaining opening to his final role, but tragedy was soon to follow.

This final role involved appearing in a cage with first one and then a pair of lions at Skegness Amusement Park. In

The Prostitute's Padre Tom Cullen explains that Davidson had always been terrified of quadrupeds, recounting his panic when jokers put a mouse into his Blackpool barrel, from which he had to be rescued. If a mouse could cause such a reaction then it must have been a huge ordeal for him to emulate Daniel by entering the lion's cage, which he used to do after addressing his audience about the inequity of his position. On the 22 July the *Lincolnshire Echo* published a story with the headline 'Ex-Rector in Lions' Den Defies Skegness Police'. The article told how he had been in 'a den of forest-bred lions' when two policemen had approached with a warrant in relation to the unpaid £7 fine, and how there had been a stand-off with Davidson refusing to leave the cage and inviting the policemen, an Inspector Harvey and his Sergeant, to enter the cage and join him. It was half an hour before he could be persuaded to leave the cage and accompany them to the station; the tenor of the article suggests that the journalist rather enjoyed the public embarrassment of the police.

28 July 1937 seemed just like any other day and, at 8.00 pm, Davidson entered the cage, as so often before, armed only with a short whip. Waiting for him were the two lions, Freddie, and the lioness, Toto. Normally his employer, a Captain Rye, would be on hand with a pole, ready to intervene if needed, but it was his day off and the only person on hand with any experience of animal training was a sixteen year old girl, Irene Somner. Eye witness accounts describe how, seeing the lions lying quietly, Davidson used his whip to encourage the lions to put on more of a show. Toto ignored the provocation but Freddie, asserting his authority, did not. He started to follow Davidson around the cage, which was not large, only about 110 square feet, while Toto simply lay

watching. Before Irene Somner could do anything about it Freddie attacked Davidson, slightly built and just 5 foot 3 inches tall, knocking him over before clamping him in his jaws by the neck and carrying him round the cage. Irene responded with both courage and presence of mind. Dashing into the cage she first tried to induce Freddie to drop his prey by pulling hard at his mane. When this failed she picked up a piece of wood and began to hit the lion about the head, at which he dropped Davidson in the far corner of the cage, near where Toto was lying. Perhaps resenting this intrusion Toto began to take an interest in the heavily bleeding victim too. Help was at hand, one customer picked up an iron bar and, assisted by the proprietor of another attraction armed with a long pole, managed to keep both animals at bay while Irene struggled to unlock another door, at the end of the cage where Davidson lay. She then pulled him out, before fainting on the spot.

Davidson, still alive but badly injured, was taken to the local Cottage Hospital, where he died two days later. His erstwhile employer had, by then, sought to make capital out of the tragedy by inviting punters to 'See the lion that mauled and injured the Rector'! A host of apocryphal tales began to emerge such as the suggestion that Davidson, on being removed from the cage, had requested that someone in the crowd should call the London papers so that the story could make the first editions.

The incident was clearly enough for Irene. She left without giving notice. Also it would seem to have given Freddie a taste for human flesh. The *Lincolnshire Echo* 20 October 1938 reports a case brought by Irene's successor, Joseph Mellin, against Captain Rye after being bitten by Freddie less than a month after the attack on Davidson.

The judge found for Captain Rye, accepting evidence that Mellin had been 'under the influence' at the time and had been stroking Freddie's nose immediately before the incident. Skegness has long claimed to be 'bracing' but in the 1930s it seems to have been too bracing, making some people susceptible to acts of foolish bravado.

The press, in reporting Davidson's death, was quite sympathetic. The *Lancashire Evening Post*, which had enjoyed the benefit of reporting on Davidson's activities in Blackpool, was notably so, indeed it was almost eulogistic, describing him as 'charming, debonair and cultured', and as a 'brilliant scholar' which might have come as a surprise to those who had known him at Whitgift or at Exeter College. It also praised his 'amazing generosity'. It even described how, with his 'charm of manner', he set out to bring a smile to the initially 'stony-faced' magistrates, his 'light-hearted quips' eventually making them smile and even laugh out loud. Evidently Chancellor North was made of sterner stuff.

Davidson's attempts to raise funds had not just depended on lions, barrels and mechanical imps. In the very week that he was de-frocked he applied for a role with the Scottish Protestant Association and later, rather bizarrely, to manage Blackpool Football Club, but the paper's claim that Davidson had given up a £1000 p.a. career on the stage for a £3 per week curacy suggests that the reporter was as susceptible to Davidson's charm as the smiling magistrates, and rather more gullible.

His family remained loyal to Davidson to the end, and beyond. His wife rushed to Skegness as soon as she heard of the incident and his children continued the fight to clear his name after his death. His funeral, at Stiffkey, was attended by an estimated 3000 mourners. No doubt many were thrill-seekers, but the whole affair was conducted with a decorum and dignity that would not have been familiar to the deceased in his later years.

It is an almost inescapable conclusion that the Church does not emerge from this case with much credit. At the very least it pursued Davidson with what seems inappropriate vigour. At worst it seems to have allowed its agents to obtain 'evidence' by very dubious means, including bribery, harassment, threats and statements made by witnesses deliberately plied with alcohol. It brought its action in the most damaging way possible and after the verdict it continued its vindictive style. The Bishop's lawyer even took to the telegraph wires to stop payment to Davidson of monies due because he was 'earning vast sums in his barrel'. It is said, but I found no evidence to substantiate the claim, that the Bishop, at the 11th hour, had second thoughts about the nature of the charges before the case was heard and wished to reduce them, but that the hour had passed by the time he tried to do something about it. If so it's a pity he didn't have those second thoughts earlier.

As for the verdict, people still argue about its correctness. At a distance of more than eighty years it is difficult to judge. But the choice of the Bishop's friend, North, to hear the case was surely inappropriate. North's judgement seems to have been based as much on inference as evidence, and the quality of much of that evidence is questionable. While it is certainly true that Davidson was foolish and naïve and was probably inappropriately attracted to young girls, the evidence adduced seems to fall some way short of proving his immorality. His antics led him to be nicknamed 'The Mormon' in some teashops, because of the number of women he entertained there, and he was banned from others for making a nuisance of himself with the waitresses. But none of this is evidence of the sort of immorality with which he was charged.

In the chapter on Davidson in *The Great Unfrocked* Matthew Parris describes Davidson as 'clearly unhinged' and a 'sex-maniac'. The Judgement of Paris belongs merely to Greek mythology and was, so the story goes, influenced by the bribes offered by the contestants. The judgement of Parris seems to ignore the inducements offered to witnesses and may be seen as a trifle harsh. The line between extreme eccentricity and insanity is narrow, and one could argue the matter either way, but I feel the evidence given in court falls a long way off demonstrating that he was a 'sex-maniac'; no witness claimed to have had full sexual relations with him. For all his failings as a parish priest the normal run of parishioners, and his family, seem to have been very fond of the Rector and supportive in his troubles, believing that his motives were simply to save vulnerable young girls from prostitution. What he may have lacked in common sense he seems to have made up in courage, not only by entering the lions' den but in being willing to incur the wrath and indignation of a formidable and frightening group of men, the pimps and protectors of the thousand or more girls he claimed to have befriended over the years. He was in many ways a sympathetic character and few could read the transcripts today without having grave doubts as to whether justice was done.

It seems appropriate as a postscript to this remarkable story to include an extract from Stanley Holloway's monologue about the visit to Blackpool by a boy called Albert and his experience with a lion called Wallace, written by Marriott Edgar some years before the tragedy.

There were one great big lion called Wallace
Whose nose was all covered with scars;
He lay in a somnolent position
With the side of 'is face on the bars.
Now Albert 'ad 'eard about lions -
'Ow they was ferocious and wild.
To see the lion lyin' so peaceful
Just didn't seem right to the child.
So straightway the brave little feller,
Not showin' a morsel of fear,
Took 'is stick with the 'orse's 'ead 'andle
And stuck it in Wallace's ear.
You could see that the lion din't like it,
For givin' a kind of a roll,
'E pulled Albert inside the cage with 'im
And swallowed the little lad - 'ole!

Canon Walter Hubert Marcon.

The Germans are not over-ettiquettish, they put their knives in their mouths and make a rare good dinner

Canon Marcon commenting on continental manners in his diary.

Canon Walter Hubert Marcon

Rector of Edgefield, committed parish priest, church builder and cyclist extraordinary.

About 76 years before I began writing these memories I was born at Edgefield on Dec. 29th, 1850, in the same room in which I now sleep, and in which I expect to die.

These are the opening words from *The Reminiscences of a Norfolk Parson* written by an extraordinary and devoted parish priest, Canon Walter H Marcon. Marcon's father and grandfather preceded him as Rectors of Edgefield, between them they clocked up a remarkable 108 consecutive years in charge of the cure of souls in that parish. Perhaps it was no coincidence that the patron of the living was Walter's uncle.

At the age of ten Walter was sent to Gresham's, then the local Grammar School. It was not an experience he enjoyed, describing in his Reminiscences a routine based on the liberal use of the cane. He tells of the Headmaster, Mr Elton—'an exceedingly severe man'—lining up a class of a dozen boys around his desk and plying them in turn with questions. Failure to answer correctly meant the boy had to hold out his hand for Elton to whack it with his cane, an action which sometimes resulted in the whole class crying at the same time. Having not started at the school until the age of 13, Walter stayed there just one year, though his younger brothers stayed there a full five. Perhaps the most surprising aspect of the story is that Walter subsequently sent his own son to the same school. It may have helped that his son was awarded an open scholarship and also that the school had changed much and was by then under the headmastership of Mr Howson, whose twenty years of stewardship turned a small Grammar into a flourishing Public School.

It was perhaps Walter's experience at a young age which led his father to advertise in the *Norfolk Chronicle* in November 1866:

> The Revd. W. Marcon B.A. (Eaton [sic] & Oxford) wishes to receive TWO or THREE BOYS, between 10 and 15 years of age, whom he could educate with his own Sons. He offers good instruction, kind treatment, and a comfortable home. Address, Revd. W. Marcon, Edgefield Rectory, Thetford, Norfolk.

It was not his first such advertisement, but one can imagine that he was not amused by the misspelling of his alma mater.

Walter, after his bad experience at Gresham's, was sent to a grammar school in Devon where, fortunately, he was caned only once—for breach of the Sabbath. He was caught responding in like manner to a bully who had 'cuffed' him. Even at this early stage he was clearly a pragmatic Christian, recording that he 'could not see the justice of putting off retaliation from Sunday to Monday'.

He finished his formal schooling at just 15 for reasons he does not explain in his reminiscences and returned to Edgefield where he took responsibility, with his father, for the education of his younger brothers before they went to

Gresham's.

His father must have been quite a hard act to follow. Educated at Eton, where he was in the XI for two seasons, he went up to Oxford, winning his cricket blue in 1843. Despite his apparent failure to take any wickets in the Varsity Match—or in his other five first class matches—he was a fast bowler of fearsome repute. No less an authority than WG Grace recorded that Marcon bowled (round arm) so fast that a delivery would 'smash a stump' if hitting it on the full, and it was said that three long stops were required when he was bowling! Grace may have had his reasons: his father, playing for Mangotsfield (a club he founded) against Lansdown, Marcon's then club, was bowled for just 1 run by Marcon in the first innings and didn't bat in the second, in which Mangotsfield were reduced to 18 for five wickets, all clean bowled by Marcon. Later, while the incumbent of Edgefield, Marcon senior played for Gunton—a two- innings match played in August 1866 resulted in a win for Gunton over Reepham, perhaps a victory ordained in heaven. The Gunton team included four clergymen, that of Reepham only two!

Despite the early termination of his schooling Marcon went up to Oxford in 1869. Again family connections may have influenced his choice, his great uncle was a Demy of Magdalen College, a form of fellowship so called because those selected were entitled to half the allowance made to Fellows. Others to hold such fellowships have included Oscar Wilde, Lawrence of Arabia, and in more recent times George Osborne. Ironically, to qualify the original requirement had been that candidates should be poor, of good morals and disposed to study.

Graduating in 1872 Walter had already determined upon a clerical career, but filled in the year before he could be ordained as a private tutor. As an aspirant curate he adopted a rather original approach. Rather than the more usual way round, he 'interviewed several clergymen' before 'finding one to my mind'. His choice fell on The Revd Grove of Govilon, near Abergavenny. This decision was later to have significance for Edgefield; Marcon recorded that he owed a large debt to Grove, not least for an introduction to one of Grove's close friends, John Dando Sedding, who later became the architect who supervised Marcon's great achievement—the transfer of Edgefield Church to a new site.

In 1879, three years after becoming Rector of Edgefield, Marcon set off on a sort of Grand Tour, stopping en route in London to fortify himself with a morning's shopping in Burlington Arcade followed by lunch at the Criterion, before setting out for Calais. His trip was of several months

duration and he recorded his impressions with daily entries in his travel diary.

These were sometimes written in ink and sometimes pencil—the latter are somewhat faded but still legible. The diary, now in a rather sorry state, is in the care of the Norfolk Record Office, and is a delightful, if sometimes discursive,

Page from Marcon's travel diary.

account of his travels, in particular in Italy. Like his fellow Norfolk clerical diarist Benjamin Armstrong, he interspersed his descriptive entries with the occasional sideswipe at continental manners—'The Germans are not over-etiquettish, they put their knives in their mouths and make a rare good dinner'. Unlike Armstrong he illuminated his descriptions with sketches; buildings, church interiors, lakeside scenes, fishermen and boats all display an almost draughtsman like talent. He describes his expeditions to many Italian cities and the sights he saw. In Venice he visited gallery after gallery and commented particularly favourably on the works of Bellini; an ironic choice of favourite as will become evident later.

He probably deserved the long holiday because by then he had already become engaged in planning an extraordinary labour of love—moving the church of St Peter and St Paul, stone by stone, brick by brick into the centre of the village and rebuilding it with the same materials.

Edgefield was one of quite a number of villages where the church was at a distance from the cottages. The reason was the Black Death. The plague caused the villagers to move to a healthier spot, leaving the church remote from the souls with whose cure the Rector was charged. In his *The Translation of a Church* published in 1928, long after the move was complete, Walter Marcon described the state of the old church when he became Rector. He remarked that since the time of the Dissolution of the Monasteries (Edgefield had come under the oversight of Binham Priory) the church had not seen any 'attention from the carpenter or the mason' until 1800 when a previous incumbent re-roofed the church, funding the cost by selling off all the lead and brasses and four of the five bells. He describes walls green with damp, rotten woodwork, pews so shabby that 'they would not be tolerated in a stable', a stained altar and, most ominously, the external walls, affected by damp in the foundations, were showing signs of collapse. A 'ruinous Lord's House' was his succinct description and one day, while in the church, he felt 'called' to act and to rebuild.

He responded to the call with astonishing energy. He quickly identified the tasks, classifying them as human, legal and financial. Change is rarely universally popular, and he was aware of some local opposition to his idea. Though many endorsed his plan, with so little movement at that time many village families went back generations and change on this scale was anathema to some. A petition was raised and sent to the Bishop calling for the retention of the status quo. Marcon recorded that the Bishop's response required a notice to be put on the door of the church advising those concerned how and where their objections could be heard. When Marcon received this response he was staying at the home of his cousin (who was to succeed his own father as patron of the parish), Wattisham Hall, near Downham Market. Marcon was delighted that the document, with its lengthy preamble in formal legal language, did not mention the means of registering opposition until the very end. He concluded that few of his parishioners would wade through all the jargon, and, persuading his cousin to take him into Kings Lynn, he hired a horse and gig with a driver and set off the 35 miles or so for home, arriving to attach the Bishop's statement to the church door just in time for Morning Service, as required by the Bishop. With an almost Machiavellian flourish he affixed the document so that the legalese was at eye level. As he had anticipated, few stooped to read the whole document, and there was little further opposition.

He had already, as soon as he felt the call, summoned what he described as 'the heads of the parish' to a meeting at the Rectory, and persuaded them, only after some

Edgefield's octagonal tower and remains of the old church.

effort, to sign a document approving the rebuilding of the Church. Approval soon followed from the Ecclesiastical Court and his next task was to raise the funds. Something in the order of £2000 was needed to carry out the scheme, and an appropriate site had to be found as well. As far as the latter was concerned he was fortunate in that the Marchioness of Lothian, who owned an estate in the village, agreed to donate a site in its geographical centre, but the raising of enough cash called for more effort. Subscriptions were sought and one of the first was for £100 from his uncle, the patron. Gradually the target was achieved.

Meanwhile he had asked JD Sedding, the architect he had met in Abergavenny, to undertake the task. Sedding was a good choice. He was a much respected ecclesiastical architect responsible for several churches, notably Holy Trinity, Sloane Street, described by John Betjeman as 'the cathedral of the Arts and Crafts Movement'. He was also the architect of St Martin's in Marple, Cheshire whose interior was designed by William Morris. Sedding also met and was influenced by Ruskin.

His task at Edgefield was unusual. First, he had to remove the roof from the old church followed by the windows and pillars and then the stones. These were all marked to ensure that they could be put back in the right order and were laid out in their correct place on the grass surrounding the church. Eventually only the unusual octagonal tower remained, as it does to this day.

It was ten years before all the stones had been brought from the old site to the new and the building finally resumed its shape, until, at last, on 14 July 1884, the Bishop of Norwich, Bishop Pelham, consecrated the church. Once all the internal work had been done, Marcon could look back with satisfaction on an extraordinary achievement.

But Marcon was not just a man on a mission to rebuild the church premises. He was as concerned with the lives and welfare of his parishioners. Initially, when returning to Edgefield as Rector, he had been concerned that the lack of lively and stimulating conversation and company might affect the quality of his life, but he came to adjust his view, as explained in his Reminiscences:

> I found life amongst bucolics very slow
> and lonely. I thought them ignorant,
> inexperienced, and wished I could transport
> them for 6 months into the Midlands where
> a daily paper was a common thing, and bring
> them back again. But I have corrected and
> abandoned this view, Ignorant they certainly
> are not, but very full of knowledge of such
> things as they were familiar with and I was
> not.

He had always sought to broaden the interests and experience of the parishioners, as a boy he had assisted his father in providing regular 'Penny Readings' for the locals which the *Norfolk Chronicle* described as 'fully appreciated by an attentive audience'. As an adult and Rector his affection for both the ways of the country at the time and the cottagers is apparent in his Reminiscences, and that affection was clearly reciprocated. One 95-year-old former parishioner undertook a fourteen mile round walk from Sheringham to enjoy refreshments with his former Rector. He was fortunate to find him at home and not either on parish business, or exploring on his bicycle, for the use of which he became renowned.

As was the way of the time the Rector was much involved in secular parish matters. Sir Diarmaid MacCulloch describes the role of contemporary clergy as 'as much local governors and social workers as spiritual pastors'. Marcon found a village with, to all intents and purposes, no school. He promptly employed an interim teacher at his own expense and sought, with limited success, subscriptions from the local 'chief residents'. When a School Board was formed by the Education Department, he became its clerk.

Housing was another of his concerns, he described many of the cottages as 'wretched hovels' with 'little accommodation for the decencies of life' and determined to do something about them. Elected to the newly formed Parish Council, he had to overcome 'difficulties, obstructions and antipathy' before new homes of satisfactory standard began to be built. His battles brought him to the attention of the Rural Housing Association who directed the gift of an anonymous donor to the improvement of other homes in Edgefield.

All this social care was undertaken in a spirit which may seem a little odd to the modern reader but which was perfectly acceptable at the time. Phrases in his Reminiscences such as 'sympathetic guidance', 'Now, the proper way with ignorance is not to blame it, but instruct it' and commendatory references to the ability of the 'women folk' to 'arrange their small treasures neatly, and keep their homes clean' are sentiments which rather have a ring of one verse in Mrs Alexander's hymn All Things Bright and Beautiful about them.

Commemoration window in Edgefield church to Canon Marcon.

> The rich man in his castle,
> The poor man at his gate,
> God made them high and lowly,
> And ordered their estate.

The sentiment implicit in this verse about social class being important, God determined and permanent so infuriated my late father that I recall him in the 1950s, when pressed by a Sunday School teacher to include the hymn in Morning Service, announcing 'We shall now sing that dreadful hymn, All Things Bright and Beautiful, omitting the silliest verse'! Despite a tone which to us today may seem a touch patronising, there can be no doubt that Marcon's efforts were motivated by nothing more than a determination to improve the lot of his parishioners and were recognised as such by them. He was a faithful, caring man who took his responsibilities seriously and discharged them remarkably effectively.

Brief reference was made before to his renown as a cyclist. In Edgefield Church today a window commemorating the centenary of the opening of the new church has a panel showing Marcon, dressed in clerical garb reminiscent of depictions of Chesterton's Catholic Father Brown, riding

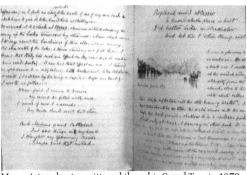

Marcon's travel notes written while on his Grand Tour in 1879.

a bicycle. He delighted in the development of the cycle and claimed in his Reminiscences to have ridden, 'with the exception of the Otto' (a peculiar machine comprising two large wheels between which the rider sat on a seat suspended between them, steering with the aid of handles which disengaged the drive from one wheel when held) 'every make of bicycle, high and low, with tyres wooden, solid, and pneumatic, from their first appearance'. By way of social commentary he suggests that in the 1860s the machines were not seen as 'suitable transport for a gentleman'. This did not deter him, he cycled just about everywhere. A trip to the continent? Well, take a couple of days cycling from Edgefield to pick up the ship at Harwich. At home? Well, Land's End, the Welsh mountains and the lakes of Scotland were all within his range. A wider choice of destinations? Well, why not ride in France, Belgium and Germany? He must have travelled very light!

While on his long mini Grand Tour of 1879, Walter had mused in verse, about the relative charms of Venice and Milan as a place to visit if he acquired a wife. While visiting the Italian lakes he wrote:

> Perplexed am I at Como
> To know which place is best
> I'd better bide a bachelor
> And let t'other thing rest

but in 1883 he married Sarah Hatherall, the daughter of a retired tradesman, in Cheltenham. Strangely she doesn't merit a mention in his Reminiscences, in fact there are very few references to his family in that work, and those that there are refer to his father and his siblings rather than his own children. The nearest he comes to any reference to Sarah is when in discussing new homes built to replace some of the crumbling cottages for the local labourers he says that he 'and the ladies of the house' would gladly exchange their old Rectory for one of them. He and Sarah had four children, three daughters and a son, born between 1885 and 1889. It is the youngest child, Grace, who is of particular interest. She was sent to board at a tiny school at 1 Park Road, Cromer run by Grace Pollard who, with one assistant, taught at the time of the 1901 census, half a dozen boarding pupils. At the time of the previous census, in 1891, the family had employed a governess.

Grace became quite a well-known character, though under an alias, Frieda (sometimes Freda) Graham. She was a leading suffragette, and no stranger to the courts. In 1913 she was twice bound over to keep the peace. In August at Bow Street she was charged with obstruction following a scuffle in Whitehall, when she was one of a group with Mrs Pankhurst demonstrating at a rally organised by the

Grace Marcon on Suffragette duty in Norwich.

Free Speech Defence Committee. Just two months later she was charged, at Westminster Magistrate's Court, with obstruction and assault. Her 'binding over' so soon after the previous sentence seems unexpectedly gentle. But her freedom was short-lived.

On 22 May 1914 she visited the National Gallery. Once inside she removed a hammer she had been hiding under her coat and proceeded to hit out at the paintings in the gallery she was in. Whatever her father's views on her behaviour, and there is no clue in his memoirs, he would surely have been disappointed that of the five paintings to which she caused particular damage three were by his favourite, Bellini. She appeared in court at Bow Street again the same day and re-appeared two days later. She didn't seem anxious to co-operate with the court, refusing, the *Daily Herald* reported, to take any interest in the case, staying silent and turning her head away when asked to plead. A plea of 'Not Guilty' was inferred but the case was found to be proved. Grace then addressed the jury saying, in not unfamiliar suffragette-speak, that her action was 'a protest against the illegal and unconstitutional action of King George in refusing to receive a perfectly legal and constitutional deputation of women'. She went on to describe this as 'an incitement to militancy'.

Her comments cut no ice with the jury and she was sentenced to six months imprisonment and was held in Holloway. It was perhaps inevitable that she should promptly decide to go on hunger strike, and she was released early, under the terms of the Cat and Mouse Act, in a pretty poor state. She had one more recorded encounter with the police. After her discharge from prison her health was very poor as a result of her hunger strike. But the suffragettes looked after their own and she was accommodated in what was, effectually, a Field Hospital for the care of those suffering from the after effects of hunger or force-feeding. This was in a house in Camden Hill Square.

On 13 June 1914, under the headline **POLICE BREAK INTO FURIES' STUDIO** the *Daily Mirror* reported that Special Branch had broken into the house by breaking the dining room window after placing a cordon of police around the house. They must have been disappointed, Freda Graham was the only occupant apart from two nurses who were looking after her. They missed the larger fry—apparently Mrs Pankhurst had previously been treated there on a number of occasions. The press report went on to say that while two detectives had entered Freda's room they 'had taken care not to disturb her', and that 'documents which are regarded as being of great importance to the police were seized'. After all this excitement she went to Canada, and there married Victor Scholey, the photographer, who had originally recorded the Sidney Street siege. Later she returned to Norfolk as a single parent during the decade of her father's death, the 1930s.

Walter Marcon continued as Rector of Edgefield until his death in 1937 having clocked up sixty-one years in the role. His time in the village saw immense changes in country life, not all of which met with his approval but he was certainly in the vanguard of efforts to improve the lot of the rural poor and his popularity with his flock is not surprising. He was clearly a man not just of faith and compassion but also of great character and energy. One suspects he would have been fun to know.

> *Everyone is interested in pigeons*

From Elwin's letter to Charles Darwin advising him to publish a book on pigeons rather than *On the Origin of Species*.

The Revd Whitwell Elwin

Rector of Booton, Editor, Writer and Church Builder

Whitwell Elwin was born in 1816 in Thurning and attended Paston Grammar School before going up to Gonville & Caius College, Cambridge, from which he graduated BA in 1839, the year of his ordination. He became a curate in a Somerset parish. According to a review published in the Spectator a few years after his death he did not take Orders as a result of any calling, but rather in the expectation that he would be instituted into the living of Booton, the patronage of which was in the family. There is a suggestion that he had been intended for the law, but changed to the Church as a means of securing an earlier income as he wished to marry his cousin, Frances. He did marry her but another cousin, Caleb, who was both Patron and Rector at Booton refused to play ball by resigning and Elwin had to wait until Caleb died, ten years later, before becoming Rector. His ancestry is romantic. He was reputedly descended from Pocahontas, the Native American princess, by her marriage to the English settler John Rolfe, a tobacco planter who came from an old Norfolk family and had been born in Heacham.

By the time he came to Booton Elwin had already made his mark in literary circles with an article in *The Quarterly Review*. This was an extremely influential journal, which was to play a major part in Elwin's life. Established in 1809 by the London publishing house of John Murray, it was intended to provide a Tory response to the Whig supporting *Edinburgh Review*. It was the brainchild of the then Foreign Secretary (and later Prime Minister) George Canning, and pursued a moderate reforming line, advocating, for example, the gradual abolition of slavery and a more humanitarian approach to the insane and the criminal.

Elwin's initial dealings were with its third editor, Lockhart, a man noted for his ten-volume biography of his own father-in-law, Sir Walter Scott. When Lockhart resigned in 1853, as a result of ill health and a series of family bereavements, Elwin was appointed Editor. He was the preferred candidate of Lockhart, who described him to Murray as 'a valuable literary acquisition'. Although Lockhart, shortly before his retirement, expressed some reservation on the grounds of the distance between Booton and London he felt that Elwin would 'be the fittest Editor of The Quarterly Review as soon as the old one drops down'. The reservation was understandable, not only was Booton remote, but at the time it did not even have a Post Office. Reputedly, Booton only acquired its first post-box as a result of Elwin's voluminous correspondence. Elwin as Editor used to travel regularly to London, staying there as each edition approached publication. The remoteness may not have worried John Murray; he too had family connections with Booton.

Elwin, although he had a house in the village, decided to build a Rectory as none existed, and this was funded by the dowry Frances had brought to the marriage. In the way that he furnished the Rectory one can detect the first signs of the eccentricity that reached maturity in his extraordinary rebuilding of the Church of St Michael and All Angels, which he undertook beginning in 1876.

The Rectory was, externally, conventional enough. He employed an architect, a profession with whose skills he was later to dispense when he turned his attention to the church. Built in the neo-Jacobean style with mullioned windows it was a substantial and attractive house. The site was a little less than ideal, being extremely boggy, and the internal decoration was eccentric in the extreme. The walls of the rooms were neither painted nor papered, the floors were not carpeted, and the windows were not provided with blinds. Creature comforts were not important to Elwin, nor it would seem to Frances, whom he had married while still at Cambridge. The family, it was recorded at the time, lived mainly in the attics, leaving the large reception rooms for the entertainment of his many influential friends.

When at Booton, he seems to have lived frugally, disdaining the heavy diet of the time and settling for a breakfast of bread and butter and a simple two course dinner. Unusually for a Victorian country parson he kept no horse, generally seen as an essential tool of the job in a rural parish. He indulged in no sport and had no hobbies beyond his literary interests, though he was fond of his domestic pets. *The Spectator*, in 1903, quoted from a letter Elwin had written in which he explained that he was having to hold the writing paper in his hand 'because he could not disturb the parrot on his leg and the "junior cat" on his lap'.

For all his idiosyncrasies he seems to have been a fairly well-loved pastor despite his frequent absences in London. As a 'squarson' he dutifully discharged his obligations in the village, even enlisting in the Volunteers in the 1850s when the fear of the French was at its height. Fond though he was of his parishioners, he was not blind to their failings. Writing to his son, Philip, in 1866 he added a postscript:

> Lewis the carrier has been sentenced to three weeks imprisonment. It might have been three months, but I hope the three weeks will have the effect of stopping his trade and will save any more poor horses from being cruelly murdered by him.

The main content of the letters he wrote to his son tended to be less prosaic. They often focussed on philosophy—Philip was reading Moral Sciences at Cambridge. Reputedly his sermons, apparently normally delivered forcefully but with his eyes closed, attracted people from outside the parish but were not so appealing to the local labourers in the village, perhaps they were a little sophisticated for locals in an area where Methodism was so strong. His benign manner was not universally observed and a handwritten note in the files at the Norfolk Record Office claims that one of his successors described him as being, on occasion, 'a tyrant in the parish' and refusing to visit one old lady on her death bed because he believed her to have been a sinner.

His circle of correspondents was far wider than simply family. He was in correspondence with such luminaries as Dickens, Scott and Thackeray, some of whose letters to Elwin are held in the Norfolk Record Office. They display great affection and Thackeray habitually addressed Elwin as Doctor Primrose, after the country clergyman in Goldsmith's Vicar of Wakefield. Thackeray was perhaps the closest of Elwin's literary friends, and one to whom he often gave advice. His admiration for Thackeray was immense. He described him as one of the three people he had known 'whose genius seemed to tower above that of the rest of mankind'. His son, Warwick Elwin, subsequently said that of the three (the others were Macaulay and Brougham) Thackeray was his father's favourite. Indeed Elwin set out to write a biography of Thackeray, but this was unfinished at his death, although the early chapters were published posthumously in *The Monthly Review*. Thackeray was a man who sometimes suffered from a lack of confidence and Elwin was a reliable source of encouraging advice and positive reviews. In a letter to his wife during one of his editorial trips to London Elwin describes a dinner party which was a disappointment 'because Thackeray was 'silent and apparently out of spirits'. Thackeray gave Elwin a lift home in his carriage and, when they were alone, had explained that he was distressed at discovering that Dickens had been behind some public criticism of him. Elwin's letter to Frances went on to record that 'Thackeray says that Dickens is mad, in which opinion I think he is not far wrong'. His letters to his wife were affectionate in salutation but largely comprised reports of his conversations with the great and good at various dinners. In one letter he describes his conversation with General Sir William Napier on the relative merits, as military commanders, of Hannibal and Marlborough, whom both regarded as more effective commanders than Wellington. In another he discusses the relative merits of Peel and Pitt as speakers in the House.

In addition he had an extensive correspondence with a number of young girls, a circle which came to be known as his 'blessed girls'. One of them Lady Emily Lutyens, a granddaughter of Bulwer Lytton, published, many years later, her correspondence with Elwin. She told how, from the age of 13 until her engagement to Lutyens in her early 20s, she had written to him almost daily, and how his advice had helped her in those years. Nothing in my research has suggested that there was any suspicion of impropriety in his relationship with this circle of young women, but Lady Lutyens does make reference to

Frances having 'suffered a good deal for the 'blessed girls".
Despite this she records that Elwin was entirely devoted
to his wife. She describes him as 'having a genius for
friendship, especially with members of the opposite sex'.
Since there was a huge age gap between Elwin and his
young lady correspondents, 58 years in the case of Lady
Lutyens, it is almost surprising that there seems to have
been a total lack of innuendo extant at the time. It should
be remembered that such correspondence was usually
carried out with the full knowledge of the parents of the
girls; it seems reasonable to assume that the relationships
were innocent enough.

The legibility of his letters is distinctly variable, those to
his wife are much harder to decipher than those to others.
The sheer scale of his correspondence is remarkable for
one who was not only short-sighted but refused to wear
spectacles. One correspondent describes Elwin writing
away with his face so close to the paper that one eye
appeared to be touching it.

He was, as an Editor, quite idiosyncratic, and occasionally
neglectful. Submitted manuscripts could lie unopened
for months; his own son described his neglect of business
matters, suggesting that Elwin was in agreement with the
remark attributed to Lord Hertford that 'a man is a fool
if he answers a letter'! Even the Bishop complained that
his letters to Elwin were rarely answered. Despite that he
proved effective at eliciting contributions from such as
Gladstone and Cecil, as well as writing over forty reviews
himself. While he must have been a frustration to John
Murray the publisher, who attempted, without success,
to persuade him to move to London to facilitate the
production of the magazine, they remained firm friends.
It was Murray who sent Elwin a pre-publication copy of

On the Origin of Species, for comment. Elwin commented at length and asked that his thoughts be passed on to Darwin.

He seems to have been sympathetic to Darwin's theory of evolution, not a position adopted by most clergy. However, he felt that Darwin had not produced sufficient evidence to prove his theory and that its credibility would suffer as a result. While warm in his praise of Darwin's observation and erudition he felt that a more convincing case could be made by examining the origins and development of one species as a precursor for the greater work. He suggested instead that Darwin should publish his observations on pigeons and simply flag up the thought that the same theory might have a wider application, and then publish his magnum opus when he could cite more positive proof.

Darwin appears to have been unimpressed by the argument, though he acknowledged its receipt with courtesy, and publication went ahead.

Elwin's place as an icon of the literati seems secure. When he relinquished the editorship of The Quarterly Review, perhaps tired of amending and correcting the work of other writers, he continued to write himself, publishing five volumes on the works of Pope, and compiling a selection of the poems and letters of Byron, both published by John Murray.

But if such accomplishments are recognised in literary circles it is for something entirely different that he is best remembered in Norfolk. In 1876, possibly as a distraction from the deaths of three of his children, he embarked on the task of creating in Booton an extraordinary Gothic church on the site of its medieval predecessor. This was an age in which wealthier clergy frequently 'improved' their churches, although the 'improvement' has not always been seen as such by later generations. But Elwin's plans were on a Titanic scale. He decided to visit churches and cathedrals all around the land to seek inspiration for his task. He did not employ an architect but on his travels he was sometimes accompanied by one of those 'blessed girls' who had for so long formed part of his circle of correspondence. He took with him a sketch book and there are a few examples of the sketches he made in a notebook held at the Norfolk Record Office.

He certainly cast his net wide. Glastonbury Abbey was the inspiration for the West door, Lichfield Cathedral, Temple Balsall in Warwickshire and St Stephen's Chapel Westminster all contributed to the design of windows. These windows all feature stained glass, and, as is appropriate for a church dedicated to St Michael and All Angels, these depict angels. Many of the models are said to have been members of his group of 'blessed girls'. Nearer to home the hammer-beam roof takes its inspiration from the church at Trunch. But outside the design is Elwin's own. A minaret stands between two extraordinarily slender towers, in some ways drawing more perhaps from his overseas travels than his tours of English churches. Overall it is far from the traditional country Norfolk church. It drew comment at the time; Lutyens was said to have described it as 'naughty, but built in the right spirit'. Today it draws comment too, perhaps best summed up by the words of the Churches Conservation Trust, in whose care the church now is—'You may love the church; you may be outraged by it, but you cannot remain unmoved by such an exuberant oddity'.

The task of rebuilding the church took up the rest of Elwin's life; it was completed just prior to his death on

January 1st, 1900. He was a true nineteenth century man. He would no doubt have been sad to see his masterpiece or his folly, depending on one's view, cease to be a place of worship half a century or so after the work was completed, but he would surely have revelled in the interest still shown in it and the care taken in its preservation.

Elwin was certainly an eccentric, but a very gifted one. He seems, as was his wife, to have been wholly without interest in material comfort, despite a high level of personal wealth. Visitors used to complain that they were expected to eat off broken crockery! Even after the costs of rebuilding the church his estate at death was a little over £32,000, equivalent to about £3,000,000 today. His wife, Frances, shared his literary interests and much of the evidence of, for example, his relationship with Thackeray is derived from her written observations. His two surviving sons both followed their father into the church, one publishing, in 1903, a book entitled *An Editor and Biographer of the last Reign, The Revd Whitwell Elwin*.

Remember, Henry, I have the housemaid,
you can have the cook

Arthur Loftus talking to his manservant after viewing the
charms of his new maidservants hired from a Boston brothel.

The Revd Arthur Loftus

Rector of Fincham, who sued his wife for the restitution of conjugal rights and was later 'deprived of his preferment' for lewd and indecent behaviour.

'The charges proved against this reverend gentleman were of the most coarsely profligate nature; intercourse with prostitutes, frequenting houses of bad fame, obtaining his domestic servants from a notorious procuress, and sharing them with his footman.' So read the headline in *The Political Examiner* on 20 December 1845.

The following year was a busy one for actions under the 1840 Church Discipline Act. In a report to the House of Commons on 25 September 1846 it was recorded that no less than fourteen had been taken against members of the clergy. Of those, two had been found 'not proven', two others were as yet undetermined. The rest had been found proved.

The variety of offences, and punishments, was wide, from 'brawling in church' which resulted in an eight month suspension from his role for The Revd Langley, through 'refusing to bury a corpse' incurring a three month suspension for The Revd Henslowe, to even more significant charges. The Revd Hurst, for 'profane cursing and swearing, lewd and indecent conversation and adultery or incontinence' received a three year suspension, his subsequent readmission to his benefice being dependent upon the production of 'a certificate of good behaviour and morals during suspension, signed by three beneficed clergymen'.

The use of these certificates was obviously quite usual in church discipline cases, including those of sexual misbehaviour. Another three year suspension with the requirement for a certificate at the end of it was handed down to The Revd Day 'for habitual and excessive drunkenness, and having been convicted of an assault' which rather begs the question as to what level of drunkenness the Court of Arches regarded as 'not excessive'. The Revd Cresswell received an eighteen month suspension and the requirement of a certificate of good behaviour for 'quarrelling, fighting, habitually swearing, frequenting public houses and intoxication'.

Some cases attracted more significant penalties. The Revd Heathcote was de-frocked for 'having been convicted of an assault with an intent to commit an unnatural crime'. But undoubtedly the most extraordinary story relates to the case of a Norfolk parson, The Revd Arthur Loftus, Rector of Fincham, and Vicar of Helhoughton, who was 'deprived of his preferment' on the grounds of 'lewd and indecent conduct and conversation, adultery, fornication or incontinence'.

Arthur Loftus had been born in 1795 into an extremely well-to-do and distinguished family. His father, General William Loftus, having been a member of the Irish parliament later became MP for Great Yarmouth, then for Tamworth, and then again for Yarmouth, all under the patronage of the Townshend family. He was successively Governor of Dumbarton Castle and Lieutenant of the Tower of London, as well as being Colonel of the Dragoons, having fought in the American War of Independence. Arthur's mother, the General's second wife, was Lady Elizabeth Townshend, daughter of the 1st Marquess

Townshend. Arthur was the third of nine children of this union, his father having had four other children with his first wife, who died in 1786.

Raised in the higher echelons of society, Arthur Loftus was educated at Clare College, Cambridge, graduating BA in 1819, and gaining his MA in 1822, the year in which he became Vicar of Fincham, at the age of 27. It was fourteen years later that he married Mary Anne Ray Clayton, in 1836. Parish records at Fincham list the births of children, a daughter in 1837, who died in infancy, a son in 1839 and a daughter born the following year who died at the age of fifteen.

The marriage was clearly not without its problems, for Arthur, just two years after the birth of his last child, brought an action against his wife for restitution of conjugal rights. *The Times* reported that the case caused great interest because of 'the known respectability of the parties'. Mrs Loftus, the paper reported, 'having left her husband without any apparent cause at the time, and, having refused to return, the suit was commenced by her husband'. Mrs Loftus had argued that she had left because of her husband's violence during her pregnancies, of which the principal evidence was the testimony of her mother. Amongst the incidents cited was Arthur's inclination to refer to the social inferiority of his wife's family; on one occasion he was said to have told her maid that she was socially superior to her mistress, at which point Mrs Loftus left him in the middle of the night, though they had subsequently been briefly reconciled.

Strangely the correspondence during their separations, while reflecting his disregard for her family did suggest that Mary Anne still felt great affection for her husband. On 1st January 1838 she wrote to him 'with the exception of speaking as you are aware you have always done of my father and mother, you have always been most affectionate and kind to me. I wish you a happy New Year, my dear Arthur, and many added to it'. Six months later she wrote 'My Dear Arthur, thank you for your kind note, most willing I am that the past should be forgotten, so no more on the subject'. She went on to encourage him to stay in Cromer where the sea air would do him good. But the issue of his attitude to her family would not go away. 'I cannot sit by when either of my parents is spoken of disrespectfully. It is true we cannot boast of the descent of a Loftus or a Townshend, but I am not ashamed of my family' she wrote later.

At the restitution hearing the Judge was dismissive of the other evidence brought on Mary's behalf on the grounds that it was unsafe as it emanated from previous servants of the couple who had fallen out with Arthur and were currently in the employ of Mary. For Arthur no less than eighteen witnesses were called to refute the allegation of violence. Five of them were servants still in his employ and another twelve were his relations. The other witness was the family doctor who described the couple as having been on affectionate terms on the very day that she left him for the final time. All attested that Arthur had been uniformly kind to his wife and, although the Judge criticised some of Arthur's language, on 13 November 1841 judgement was given in his favour, his mother-in-law's evidence having been felt 'to entertain a prejudice against her son-in-law'. His wife was admonished and instructed to return to the marital home. She didn't. Given the relative warmth of Mary Anne's correspondence with her estranged husband it does seem possible that a major contributor to their final separation may have been a bad case of 'mother-in-law's tongue'.

Loftus was clearly a man of considerable physical appetite, though what he got up to in the fourteen years he was at Fincham prior to his marriage is a mystery. After it became clear that Mary Anne was not planning to return he consulted his doctor, Dr Arthy, complaining that the deprivation of sexual activity was making him ill. The doctor reportedly suggested to him that he should seek such gratification elsewhere, implying that a discreet relationship at a distance might meet the case. Loftus asked him whether, if he were discovered, the doctor would give a certificate to the effect that such activity was essential for Loftus' continued good health, and he had agreed, though thinking of the request, as he later said, as little more than a joke.

Unfortunately, discretion does not seem to have been a part of Loftus' character, at least as far as sexual activity was concerned. At the time he employed a valet called Henry Twiddy; the 19th century equivalent of the red top press gilded the lily a little bit by describing him as either a footman or a butler. He and Loftus clearly both felt the lack of female company in the Rectory, at which there also lived the curate, a Mr Balls. For a year, between October 1843 and September 1844 Loftus and Twiddy were alleged to have become regular attenders at the house of a Mrs Sconce, just 12 miles away at King's Lynn. This was a 'house of assignation' and according to the Articles (charges) at the later court hearing, they travelled there weekly to commit adultery or fornication. The Articles went on to allege that the pair extended their custom to a brothel in Boston, run by a Mrs Foreman. It was Mrs Foreman, the charges read, who at the 'express instance' of Loftus engaged two prostitutes, Jemima Cross and Susan Warsop to enter his service in 'the ostensible capacities of housemaid and cook'.

Soon there was rumour in the village, no doubt compounded when, within two weeks of the girls' arrival, the Reverend Balls moved out of the Rectory first into lodgings and soon out of the parish altogether. Perhaps the tipping point came when Jemima became pregnant. A miscarriage was effected with the help of Susan, but it was at about that time that Loftus, presumably concerned that this too would become the subject of village gossip, arranged for Jemima to leave his service. He provided her with a reference which, while brief, was positive and obviously made no reference to her extra-curricular activities while a member of his household. That left a shortage in the distaff side of Rectory residents, a situation quickly remedied with the assistance of the reliable Mrs Foreman, who sent a girl called Maria Ward to take Jemima's place.

But the time of retribution drew near. The increasing amount of gossip about the goings on at the Rectory reached the ears of Mrs Loftus' friends, and soon those of the Bishop, who summoned Loftus to attend him on the 3 September 1844. Whatever the Bishop said to Loftus certainly galvanised him, he went home and sacked Susan and Maria on the spot. Loftus, it appeared from the judge's later remarks, had effectively thrown himself on the Bishop's mercy, asking to be allowed to retain £200 p.a. of his stipend. The Bishop was clearly not satisfied with the answers given to him by Loftus and established an enquiry which determined that the matter should be referred to the ecclesiastical courts.

Loftus denied everything, producing testimonials from local clergy and gentry asserting that he was of good character. He was also familiar with the courtroom, having been a Justice of the Peace for many years.

E.E. Groom, Mileham & C? Litho.

St MARTIN'S CHURCH,
FINCHAM.

St. Martin's Church, Fincham (1863).

Published in Revd Blyth's 'Historical Notices & Records of the Village & Parish of Fincham in the County of Norfolk'.

When the matter reached the court in 1846, the Judge in the case was Sir Herbert Jenner Fust. Loftus chose as his counsel Dr Jenner, the Judge's son.* Jenner-Fust was by this time in his late 60s and sufficiently infirm to require the help of two 'footmen' whose role was to carry him into the court. The Judge decided that the nature of the evidence was so shocking that the court should hear the case without the proceedings being open to the public.

The depositions of the various witnesses when the case came to court in 1846 need to be considered with caution. The Judge was dismissive of much of the evidence and several times criticised those who had recorded it, actually alleging that the purpose had been to create a prejudice against Loftus. The deposition of Jemima Cross is particularly interesting, as she describes life at the Rectory in detail. In December 1843 she and Susan

Warsop had come to live at the Rectory, having been sent the money necessary to pay their fares from Boston. On arrival she and Susan joined Henry Twiddy, and later Loftus, in the pantry for a chat. Loftus had, she said in evidence 'kept talking to us about his wife, saying she had left him and how uncomfortable he was without her'. She described how Loftus had then asked which of them was the cook and which the housemaid. Before leaving their company he had said to Twiddy 'Remember, Henry, I have the housemaid, you can have the cook'. Twiddy then took Susan to bed, but Jemima slept in her own room. The next morning Loftus allegedly enquired of her why she had not come to his room and arranged that she should do so that night. According to her deposition he, later in the day, gave her money to purchase plainer frocks, as he was afraid the gay nature of her own clothes might give rise to suspicion in the village that she was no ordinary housemaid. From then on she slept with Loftus every night for about a month, at which point Twiddy, while the worse for wear, took her to bed himself. She alleged that Twiddy and Loftus had argued about her change of partner, but that Twiddy had prevailed. It isn't difficult to imagine that Twiddy, having information which could have totally destroyed Loftus was no longer in a traditional servant/master relationship with him, and was in a position to insist on having his own way. Loftus had to console himself with Susan. Soon, all parties except the Rector had venereal disease and then Jemima Cross became pregnant, her expressed belief being that Loftus was the father. An abortion was effected by Susan administering to Jemima a concoction comprising dried laurel leaves and gin.

While confirming the situation with Jemima's pregnancy, Susan Warsop's evidence was more equivocal. She refused to confirm whether or not she had slept with Loftus, while acknowledging that she had done so with Twiddy. She said that Loftus had been a good master to her, and she wished to say nothing against him. She also appeared to have a very convenient loss of memory, being unable to recall whether Cross had slept with Loftus. The tone of her evidence doesn't suggest great affection between the two girls, perhaps she resented Twiddy's apparent preference for Jemima. She did however confirm Jemima's evidence about their first evening at the Rectory, saying that Loftus had joined Twiddy and the girls in the pantry with 'a candle in one hand and a prayer book in the other'.

Another prostitute, Hannah Payne, gave evidence that she had seen Loftus at Mrs Sconce's house of assignation in King's Lynn on four occasions in the spring of 1844, and that she had slept with him twice. As with others she gave evidence that he had told her that he was a clergyman, that his wife was not living with him, and that his doctor had 'ordered him to have women'.

Mrs Foreman confirmed that Loftus had been a visitor to her house, that he had told her that his wife had left, that he missed her and wished she would come back to him. She also attested that Loftus had asked her to procure two women to come as servants to his house. She claimed to have harboured doubts as to whether he really meant this as he had seemed confused at breakfast that day. She had subsequently received a letter from Twiddy confirming the request with which she immediately complied.

Jenner (junior) for Loftus argued that the evidence was unsafe given the nature and occupation of the witnesses. Loftus denied everything and the stack of positive evidence as to his character must surely weigh in favour of his being believed.

Giving judgement Sir Herbert said that before hearing the evidence the Court had leant to the view that the 'story of such promiscuous intercourse was so improbable that the charges defeated themselves'. However, his view had changed as he heard the evidence, and at the inference to be drawn from the failure of the defence to call as a witness The Revd Balls who had been living in the house at the time. Surely, mused the judge, he must have been aware if any of the alleged behaviour had been going on. Why was he not called to testify as to the innocence of the behaviour of Loftus? Why, he asked did Loftus, knowing the character of Cross give her a positive reference? Why had he sought to negotiate financially with the Bishop? He made the point that it was inconceivable that, at the time Loftus hired the two servants, he was unaware of their character and profession, and having reviewed all the evidence he concluded that 'it is utterly impossible to believe for one moment that Mr Loftus was ignorant of the proceedings going on at his house'. While he accepted that the evidence of the character of Loftus came from very respectable witnesses, including the Rural Dean, he 'would be glad to know' whether had any of the gentlemen giving such evidence been aware of the evidence that Loftus had engaged prostitutes as servants, that three residents in the Rectory had contracted venereal disease, that a miscarriage had been procured for one of the girls and that Loftus, knowing all this, had given her a good character, they would still have believed him innocent. In any event, the Judge concluded, while evidence of character could be decisive in cases where there was doubt, such was not the case here.

He went on to sentence Loftus to deprivation of any preferment he possesses either in the diocese of Norwich or elsewhere in the province of Canterbury. He added that 'it is quite impossible that he should be suffered to remain in possession of any preferment'.

The punishment, and some others by the Court of Arches, caused something of a scandal. *The Times* on 16 December 1845 referred to the lack of 'efficient punishment of offenders among the spiritual body, at least effectual provision'. The article went on to say that although the Church should always be held in veneration, and the paper 'never without pain' found itself 'compelled to cast discredit on her ministry', the leniency of some recent sentences was an 'abuse' to which the maximum publicity should be given. It's point, in relation to the Loftus case, was that instead of 'degradation' i.e. de-frocking, the sentence had been simply that Loftus was to be deprived of any preferment in the Diocese of Norwich or the province of Canterbury. Put simply it was open to any Bishop in a Diocese not within that province immediately to induct Loftus to the care of souls in a new living. This it described as 'a mockery', asserting that he should have been 'ignominiously expelled' from his sacred office. It wasn't the judge's leniency that was the issue, but rather the limits of authority enjoyed by the Court in isolation to pass such a sentence. Perhaps it was that at which Jenner-Fust was hinting in the final sentence of the previous paragraph.

Looking at the whole picture, perhaps the most illuminating part of Jemima's evidence had been that she claimed that Loftus talked a great deal about his wife, and how much he missed her. Had he simply been after sexual gratification then surely it would have been simpler, and certainly less embarrassing, to have brought no action for the restitution of conjugal rights and simply to have availed himself of the delights available both

THE RECTORY HOUSE,
FINCHAM.

The Rectory House, Fincham (1863).

Published in Revd Blyth's 'Historical Notices & Records of the Village & Parish of Fincham in the County of Norfolk' published in 1863. His description records: 'The RECTORY HOUSE is old, but commodious and well built. It consists of three stories, with high-pitched roofs and gables. By a date on the large central chimney, in one of the attic chambers, it appears to have been built, or rebuilt, in the year 1624. It presents a handsome front to the north, and is well situated, with its garden and glebe lands on the south.'

in the brothels of King's Lynn and Boston, and later in the convenience of his own home. Evidence from Mrs Foreman and from one of the prostitutes at King's Lynn shows the extent to which he ignored Dr Arthy's advice about discretion. At both houses of assignation he made no secret either of his profession or of the fact that he was separated from his wife.

It is difficult to conclude that Loftus was anything other than an inappropriate character for a clergyman and that he was either unable or unwilling to control his physical desires. At the same time it is difficult not to feel a little sorry for him. It seems clear that, for all his snobbish view of her family background, he was genuinely fond of his wife. The evidence of his doctor, of Mrs Foreman and especially of Jemima's first evening at Fincham all suggest that. Perhaps had his mother-in-law been less determined to keep him and his wife apart, he might have behaved differently. His family appears to have disowned him, so successfully that the Peerage website suggests that he died soon after the case, c 1847. Other sources suggest that he lived to a ripe old age, dying in 1884.

In the church of St Martin's Fincham, when visited by the author in December 2018, there was a display headed 'Times Past'. It is perhaps not surprising that while there is reference to Loftus' predecessor and to his successor, The Revd Blyth, whose devoted 40 year incumbency must have done much to restore the local reputation of the Church, Loftus is notable only by his absence. His name on the list of incumbents hanging in the church is the only visible sign that this extraordinary man was ever responsible for the cure of souls in the parish.

* Dr Jenner had a Norfolk connection. He was a fine cricketer, playing at Eton and captaining Cambridge University. He was an all-rounder in every sense of the word. He was a good batsman, but when his side were in the field he not infrequently bowled at one end while keeping wicket during the intervening overs from the other! In those days, of course, pads were not worn. He played for Norfolk in 1831, scoring 118 against Essex, in a match played at Swaffham, and was probably a contemporary in the Norfolk team of the father of Canon W H Marcon (qv). He was President of the MCC in 1833.

Revd George Smith.

*All right Mister, you do the praying and I'll send the black b******** to Hell as fast as I can.*

Reported response of a private, when admonished for swearing by Chaplain George Smith, during the battle of Rorke's Drift, January 1879.

The Revd George 'Ammunition' Smith

of Docking, Norfolk—Hero of Rorke's Drift

Ask anyone on the Cromer omnibus to name a Norfolk hero and the chances are they'd say 'Nelson'. Press for a second and, after a pause for reflection, the names Edith Cavell or Coxswain Henry Blogg might be mentioned. It's very unlikely George 'Ammunition' Smith would be brought up. Yet The Revd George Smith, a native of Docking in West Norfolk, was also a true hero.

His claim to hero status comes not from a long and sustained series of actions, but from his courage on one violent and bloody day in January 1879 when no less than eleven Victoria Crosses were awarded as about 100 British soldiers beat off a force of nearly 4000 Zulu warriors at the Mission Station called Rorke's Drift. To their eternal shame the makers of that otherwise excellent film 'Zulu' simply airbrushed Smith out of the story in which he had played such an heroic part. Contemporary and more recent artists have, in their paintings of the siege, been more generous. Padre Smith features prominently in the famous paintings by both de Neuville and Lady Elizabeth Butler and in the 1990 painting by American artist Keith Rocco. Judging by the accounts offered by survivors this prominence was well deserved.

Advancing against the Zulus, the British Commander in Chief, Lord Chelmsford, had left a small detachment of men on guard at Rorke's Drift mission station, in temporary use as a military hospital. Including the patients, the total British contingent amounted to just over 100, and was in a district nominally under the command of Major Spalding, one of Chelmsford's staff officers. Reinforcements were expected imminently from the nearby base at Helpmekaar. Rorke's Drift was an essential crossing point of the Buffalo River in order for Chelmsford to continue his advance into Zulu territory and he ordered a small party of Royal Engineers to move up to there to facilitate the crossing. This unit was under the command of Lieutenant Chard, who had never previously seen action. The senior officer at Rorke's Drift itself was Lieutenant Bromhead, an experienced officer whose request to begin fortifying the mission station had been turned down; he was told to leave that to the Royal Engineers when they arrived.

With them was a civilian, George Smith, the Rector of Estcourt, who had agreed to act as Chaplain to the Volunteers marching with Chelmsford. Smith, the son of the village shoemaker in Docking, was a very noticeable, and somewhat eccentric, figure, standing well over six feet tall, slightly stooped, with a massive red beard and habitually dressed in a frock coat tinged green with mildew. Having been at college in Kent, he originally went to South Africa to be a lay missionary under the auspices of the SPG (Society for the Propagation of the Gospel) but had subsequently been ordained. Little is known of his childhood, though Canon Lummis MC, in his account of Smith's life (see Bibliography), suggests that he may have been a sickly child, drawing this inference from the fact that the Baptismal records of St Mary's Church, Docking show that he was baptised the day after his birth on the 8 January 1845. Such early baptism was the norm in those less secular days when it was thought unlikely that an infant would survive. By the time of the defence of Rorke's Drift, two weeks to the day after his 35th birthday, any doubts about his physical condition lay behind him. He was the embodiment of the 'muscular Christianity' which distinguished so many of the missionaries of the time.

He had been ordained by Bishop Colenso of Maritzburg, himself a former Norfolk Rector at Forncett St Mary. Colenso and Smith were very different people, the former a Low churchman imbued with a belief in equality for all regardless of race or religion, the latter of the High Church persuasion and forceful in his approach to the conversion of the Zulu people to Christianity. Smith's reports to the SPG, as quoted by Lummis, tell us something of his life in a parish where more than half the Europeans were Boers and the total European population was hugely outnumbered. They tell of his success in building a new church, though the bell tower lacked a bell and the windows lacked glass for want of funds. But they also show that Rorke's Drift was far from being Smith's first experience of the perils of colonial life. He reported how, in 1873, as the threat of rebellion grew, the church building, with stone walls and an iron roof, was to be at the centre of a defensive ring of wagons. The plan was to offer refuge to the women and children and to be, if necessary, the final retreat of the men if the wagons were overrun. The following year he was reporting how another of his churches had been pressed into use as an ammunition store—by this time the rebellion had started. He describes riding through hostile territory, staying in farms barricaded and occupied by frightened families, to offer his services to the military in the recovery and burial of those lost in an early engagement. In The Washing of the Spears, Donald Morris describes Smith as 'a fire-eater, and a rabid High Churchman' who, having 'barricaded his church as a refuge for his parishioners, rode off with the Karkloof Troop'. Smith's offer was accepted and he was part of an expedition which found the mutilated bodies of three members of the Volunteers and two native members of the troop. At 5 o'clock the following morning the bodies were interred with full 'Church and Military Honours'.

His role at Rorke's Drift was to offer spiritual comfort to the wounded in the medical care of Surgeon Reynolds and to the other men based there.

When Chard, the Royal Engineer, arrived he felt there was some ambiguity in his orders so he sought Major Spalding's permission to set off after Chelmsford's column to clarify his duties. Spalding was preoccupied, the reinforcements from Helpmekaar were overdue. He instructed Chard to select the best area for the additional troops to entrench when they arrived before he set off. Chard's departure was delayed by this duty and he eventually caught up with Chelmsford's force in the camp at Isandlwana. Having clarified his duties he returned to Rorke's Drift, worried in case the Zulus he had spotted moving in that general direction were able to cut off his return journey. It was a difficult enough route already, given the sodden nature of the ground following heavy rain, but he completed the journey without incident.

On his return he reported to Major Spalding and expressed his doubts about his ability to defend the ferry boats needed for troops to cross the river in the event of a sustained attack; he had only seven regular soldiers and about 50 native troops. Spalding, recognising this, decided to set out for Helpmekaar himself to find out the reasons for the delayed arrival of the reinforcements and to expedite their arrival. First he had to appoint either

Bromhead or Chard to command in his absence. The Army List he consulted showed that although Bromhead was the more experienced soldier, Chard, as a Royal Engineer had been commissioned as full Lieutenant on passing out, and so had held that rank for longer than Bromhead. So Chard was nominally in command for what Spalding anticipated would be a very short absence. The scene was now set and the cast selected for one of the most extraordinary sieges in British colonial history. But, before the curtain went up at Rorke's Drift, the horror of Isandlwana had to be played out.

The site of the Battle of Isandlwana.

Moving off in pursuit of the elusive enemy Chelmsford, ignoring confused intelligence reports about the approach of a large force of Zulus, had split his own force in two, leaving about 1200 in a camp at Isandlwana, a site which had been chosen despite local advice that it was not easily defendable. To make matters worse no serious attempt was made to make the camp safer, no ditches were dug, no barricades prepared—even 'laagering' (creating a ring of wagons as a protective shield), the traditional defence against Zulu attack was left undone.

The subsequent battle of Isandlwana turned into perhaps the worst, and most embarrassing, defeat suffered in the days of Empire. The disgrace was compounded by the loss of the Regimental Colours; only a handful of men survived. The dramatic attempt to save the colours by Lts. Melvill and Coghill formed a stirring start to the film, Zulu, but proved fruitless and both were killed and their bodies mutilated some five miles from the battlesite. Behind them was a scene of devastation. The Zulu attack had been brutal. Of the 1200 or so British troops at the camp only about 60 escaped.

Some have suggested that the award of 11 VCs for the action which followed at nearby Rorke's Drift was part of an attempt to disguise the ignominy and the extent of the defeat at Isandlwana by 'talking up' the heroic defence of the mission station. Even if there was an element of truth in that suggestion—one contemporary officer in South Africa described the awards as 'comical', no-one can deny that there was raw courage aplenty as the contingent, and

The site of the hospital at Rorke's Drift (1997).

the patients fought desperately to hold off an attacking force nearly 40 times their number. And George Smith was involved right from the start.

Rorke's Drift was only six miles away from Isandlwana and the sounds of battle carried there clearly.

Three men from the station rode up a nearby hill to see for themselves how things fared. George Smith was accompanied by the Swedish missionary, Witt, whose home the station had been, and the Medical Officer, James Reynolds. Even from this vantage point the camp at Isandlwana was not visible, though its environs were, especially to Smith who was the only one equipped with a telescope. Suddenly an ominous darkness descended, a partial eclipse of the sun had occurred and, as it passed, they could detect a large group of black figures coming away from the direction of the camp. They initially assumed that they were members of Chelmsford's Natal Native Contingent; they were soon to be disillusioned. The approaching men stopped and set fire to a farm. Even then the watchers continued to assume that the men were members of the Natal Natives until they came so close that the watchers could see that the two horsemen leading the advance were black, the officers of that contingent were all white. The shock must have been extreme. As Witt later reported, they were within rifle range by the time the three realised their error and they fled back down the hill to warn the defenders. There are a number of accounts as to how the warning was delivered. This is hardly surprising. When the story was told afterwards all those present had by then lived through an extraordinary experience and their minds must have been filled with memories of desperate fighting. One account has it that the three had been accompanied by a Private John Wall who shouted a description of the advancing Zulus that became famous as a symbol of the huge number of the attackers— describing them as 'BLACK AS HELL AND AS THICK AS GRASS'. Other accounts suggest that the news arrived simultaneously of a disaster at Isandlwana. On arrival at Rorke's Drift Witt promptly rode off to safety. Reynolds, one of the most deserving of those eventually awarded the VC, stayed to look after his patients. According to one version, Smith declined to flee with Witt, deeming it his christian duty to stay with the defenders. Others offer a more prosaic interpretation, that he discovered that both his horse and his bearer had disappeared, presumably together, leaving him with little choice but to see the battle out. In either case he was to play a key role in the desperate action which followed and his status as a hero is unchallenged. Chard had not been at the post when the news arrived but, summoned by Bromhead, he arrived in time to read written confirmation from officers who had escaped the battle at Isandlwana that a large force of Zulus was on its way to attack Rorke's Drift.

Very little time was available to prepare. By the time Chard arrived the building of a barricade had been started. The station was open to attack from all sides, and Chard hurriedly used his professional knowledge to make the defences as effective as possible, incorporating the existing buildings. The barricade primarily comprised barrels, mealie (maize) bags and biscuit tins from the stores. These were more substantial than they may sound. The mealie bags were sacks weighing about 14 stone, and the biscuit tins about ten stone. Two wagons were also pressed into service. The windows of the hospital building incorporated in the defence line were blocked out with mattresses, but nothing could be done about the walls outside the defence perimeter and the dead ground both of which would provide cover for the attackers. The men worked feverishly on the defences, they couldn't tell how much time they would have to prepare for the onslaught.

Realising the temptation, Chard ordered a guard to be set on the barrels of rum in the stores with strict orders to shoot any man who tried to broach them. The maintenance of morale was essential; occasionally small groups of men escaping from the massacre at Isandlwana would ride past the station in full retreat and their appearance and shouted warnings alarmed the defenders. With typical British aplomb one of those defenders, Private Hitch, decided that the small garrison deserved a cup of tea before facing the Zulu horde. The morale held, for now.

In the late afternoon the sound of rifle fire close by could be heard and some of the locally raised troops deserted the scene. One British Corporal decided to run too, but was shot by rifle fire from the camp, presumably 'pour encourager les autres'. The garrison now comprised about 100 fit men, supplemented by another 30 or so patients suffering from everything from assegai wounds to fever.

Shortly after 4 o'clock the attacks began. The British opened fire when the first wave of Zulus were about 600 yards away and although there were immense casualties the Zulus continued the attack, gradually surrounding the post so that the attack came from all sides. The hospital in particular was a hotspot. The dead ground in front of it made excellent cover for the Zulus and the battle was particularly fierce there. The fighting was desperate, and as the few defenders fought off wave after wave of attacks, it was Padre Smith who kept them supplied with ammunition. Smith in his white helmet, and carrying a haversack with ammunition, hurried from one position to the next delivering cartridges, pausing only to reprimand the men for swearing and to remind them to 'shoot low'.

Alphonse de Neuville—'The Defence of Rorke's Drift 1879'.

Based on eye witness accounts, it depicts several events of the battle occurring at once. Central to the action is Smith handing out cartridges from a haversack.

Darkness fell a little after 6pm. By then the hospital was in a desperate state. Surgeon Reynolds, delivering ammunition, had a lucky escape, a bullet passed through his helmet, just missing him. The action was so intense that the rifles overheated to the extent that the defenders could only hold them using cloths to protect their hands. Gradually parts of the hospital had to be conceded, most accounts of the battle tell of extraordinary acts of individual bravery as defenders fought hand to hand to pull the wounded out of the building which was by now ablaze and move them, taking them to the relative safety of the entrenchment established behind the biscuit boxes.

While the blazing hospital meant a difficult evacuation of the wounded, it did provide a source of light enabling the defenders better to respond to the waves of attacks. The siege lasted throughout the night, although the intensity gradually slackened after dark, enabling the defenders to conserve the ammunition Smith was delivering—just as well because it was some 12 hours before the last shots were fired, at about 4.30am the following day; by then, according to some reports less than two boxes of ammunition remained unused.

When dawn broke it was clear that the Zulus, disheartened by the level of casualties and the failure significantly to breach the makeshift barricades, had retired and preparations were made to send small patrols out to collect weapons abandoned by the attackers. This was not without risk; quite apart from armed Zulus shooting from the surrounding hills there were two incidents closer to home. Suddenly one Zulu, left behind in the general withdrawal, leapt up from within the cattle enclosure and fired his musket into the yard before making good his escape on foot. Another wounded Zulu, playing dead, tried to grab the rifle of a soldier busy collecting assegais. George Smith recorded that the patrols recovered more than 100 muskets and 400 assegais from the immediate vicinity; given that so many armed Zulus had successfully withdrawn, it seems clear that the attackers had not just been numerous, but well armed. The scale of the achievement in holding them off is clear.

George Smith was not one of the eleven recipients of the VC, despite his gallantry. A number of reasons for this have been suggested; the most likely seems to be that he was not, at the time, a member of the forces. Another explanation offered by one commentator was that Smith was given the choice of a medal or a commission as an army chaplain, and chose the latter. Although the choice sounds bizarre, and there seems no evidence to support the suggestion, he did become a full time chaplain, and later served with distinction both at home and in Egypt. He was clearly a man of some presence—no doubt his height helped. A report in the *Natal Witness* a few weeks before the events described the scene at a church parade.

> It is an impressive scene to witness 1000 warlike men, in various uniforms, form square, and join a robed priest, with a band of musicians in the worship of Almighty God. This is one of the greatest civilising influences which the forces could carry with them.

Padre Smith (nicknamed 'Daddy' by the troops) clearly took well to Army life. In The Washing of the Spears, Morris descibes him as having an 'unquenchable enthusiasm for military life'. Canon Lummis quotes the diary of a contemporary officer as describing him being 'as keen on the fight as the best of us' and, referring to his appointment as a Chaplain in these terms 'a better man they could not get. He seems to hit off all the motives and feelings of the men to a 'T'.' It would be difficult to disagree.

Smith did not marry and spent some time in his retirement travelling, but settled finally in a hotel in Preston, where his last posting had been. His friend, Lt (later Colonel) Chard VC, who with Bromhead had been in charge of the defence of Rorke's Drift, stayed for a while in the same hotel, though he died in 1897 in Somerset after a long battle against cancer of the tongue. One of his last visitors before his death was George Smith. Smith's travels took him to Australia, where he was held in special affection; de Neuville's painting of the battle had been bought by the Art Gallery of New South Wales, and it was there that Smith first saw it. The Gallery's Director at the time wrote later that Smith had been visibly moved by this reminder of the death of so many colleagues. When he died, in 1918, the Australian Press published a generous and lengthy obituary. At home, *The Times* was somewhat briefer, perhaps because just a few weeks after the Armistice at the close of 'the war to end all wars' Rorke's Drift seemed a distant sideshow.

His burial was marked by a firing party from two Lancashire regiments and the inscription on his tombstone described him as 'One of the Heroes of Rorke's Drift' and 'a brave and modest Christian gentleman'. One hopes he does indeed rest in peace, but, even though the hotel in which he lived was demolished and rebuilt, as late as the 1980s there were claims that his spirit rang the bell in the bar, and left unopened but empty bottles in the fridge, causing members of the staff there to consult a medium in search of an explanation!

> The warrant was withheld 'in consequence of the station of life of Mr Holmes'.

Clerk to Magistrate.

The Revd Edmund Holmes

one time patient and later chaplain at Heigham Hall Lunatic Asylum, Norwich, accused of attempted rape of a minor.

On 17 October 1854 a quarterly session of the City of Norwich and County of Norfolk magistrates was held under the chairmanship of the Mayor of Norwich, Sir Samuel Bignold.

At the meeting there was a motion to reappoint those magistrates who were the Visitors of Lunatic Asylums. In the normal course of events such motions were adopted almost as a matter of course, but such was not the case this time. A barrister, Nathaniel Palmer, said that he could not approve the motion without first being satisfied that the Visitors had executed their duties in a proper manner.

He referred to 'reports which have been in circulation that something very wrong had been going on in some of the Asylums' and wanted to know what the Visitors had done about it.

The reports to which he referred related to an incident a couple of years earlier, in June 1852. A Mrs Bunn, of Wymondham, had returned from church to find her 13-year-old daughter, Phoebe, lying on a bed with a clergyman 40 years her senior, The Revd Edmund Holmes. This was at the home of Mrs Bunn's sister-in-law, Hannah, who was Holmes' housekeeper. After throwing

Holmes out into the street she reported the matter to the constabulary, and Holmes was promptly brought before the local magistrate, William Cann. In the best tradition of Happy Families, the court clerk was Cann's son, William, junior. Had the case subsequently gone to trial, and Holmes been found guilty of the attempted rape of a minor he might well have hanged.

The Holmes family was wealthy and one of some distinction in Norfolk society; Edmund's older brother, The Revd John Holmes, had inherited Brooke Hall and an estate of almost 3000 acres from their father. Another sibling was the local magistrate, and two sisters had married other clergymen. Edmund himself had been educated at Corpus Christi College in Cambridge and had been a country clergyman for almost thirty years, remaining unmarried. It is possible that this family background weighed on the Magistrate's mind when considering the matter. He declined to hear the case, declaring, despite his total lack of medical qualification, that Holmes was clearly insane.

This afforded the family the opportunity to avoid the disgrace of a trial by having Edmund Holmes certified and put into an asylum without any criminal charge. This was at the time a recognised route for upper class families to hide away family members likely to cause embarrassment. The magistrate's son, William junior, when asked about the case at the subsequent enquiry, admitted that the warrant had been withheld 'in consequence of the station in life of Mr Holmes' and that probably 'had he been a poor man' the situation would have been different, and the case would have been heard first and, if the charge of sexual assault been proved, the question of Holmes' s sanity would only then have been considered.

In order to achieve this admission to an asylum it was necessary for the head of the Holmes family to do two things. First, he had to find an institution prepared to take Edmund, and then, two independent medical practitioners unconnected with the institution, had to declare the patient insane. The first was not difficult. There were several commercial institutions happy to accept the fees, which wealthy families were willing to pay, to hide away those whose behaviour might damage their good name.

John Holmes' choice fell upon Heigham Hall, an institution opened some years previously by two doctors, Messrs Nichols and Watson. Nichols set out to obtain from two independent doctors the requisite certificates to enable Edmund Holmes to be admitted as insane. This proved a bit trickier and it was partly as a result of his endeavours in this cause that the story became well known and widely reported a couple of years later. One doctor, Dr Mills, declined to supply the certificate as he had found no evidence of insanity in Holmes when he

Heigham Hall, private mental hospital.

interviewed him. But it was another local doctor, Dr Hull, who also declined a certificate, who was to create a scandal by his allegations two years after the event.

The allegations were to the effect that Nichols had sought to resort to bribery to induce Dr Hull to sign the necessary papers to certify Holmes insane as one of the independent examiners. Hull claimed that Nichols had, after Dr Mills demurred, then approached Hull. He claimed that Nichols had boasted about helping to save Holmes from the clutches of the law and gone on to say that it would be worth 'several hundreds a year' financially if Holmes was declared insane. Dr Hull had declined, he said, to have anything to do with the matter and Nichols had gone on to find two other signatories, one of whom as a resident in the village effectually owned by the Holmes family could certainly have felt under some pressure to go along with the family's wishes.

Two years after Edmund's admission to the asylum a highly respected local doctor, Dr Ranking, became a co-proprietor of Heigham Hall, and it was shortly after that appointment that Dr Hull went public with allegations of impropriety in connection with the admission of Edmund Holmes.

The matter was already the subject of local gossip, but it was Dr Hull's allegations about the case which brought national interest. What fanned the flames of rumour even more was that, according to Nichols and his colleagues, they had been so successful in their treatment of Holmes that within a couple of months this man who had been admitted as insane had been completely restored to sanity,—so much so that although he remained in residence this was on a voluntary basis and he had been appointed as Chaplain to the asylum.

There were many to whom the whole case smelled as fishy as a box of Yarmouth bloaters. Here was a clergyman, a member of a county family, caught in bed with a child, who had not been tried because an unqualified practitioner (the magistrate) had declared him insane, who had been admitted to an asylum, apparently miraculously cured in a matter of weeks and appointed to the care of souls of the inmates at the same asylum. Doubts were not unnaturally cast upon the justification for his original admission.

In fairness there was some evidence to support that admission. Holmes had behaved strangely before. His family had in fact previously referred him to Dr Nichols, who had, at that time, not seen a need for immediate admission. Both the local policeman who had arrested Holmes and Mrs Bunn the mother of the alleged victim of Holmes' advances believed him to be insane. A prominent local clergyman, The Revd William Wayte Andrew, under whom Holmes had served as a curate, disclosed a conversation in which Holmes had told him that he had been tempted to kill Mrs Bunn (aunt of the child) as she was 'possessed of seven devils', on one occasion he had attempted to choke her.

Despite the rumours, given that so many parties did indeed think Holmes insane, the matter would probably have remained simply the subject of local speculation had it not been for the intervention of Dr Hull. The fact that he made no fuss until two years after the alleged impropriety raises questions about his motivation. From the timing it appears possible that the proximate cause of his public allegations may have been the acquisition of a share in the asylum by Dr Ranking.

A week after the original magistrates' meeting the matter was considered again. Dr Hull repeated his allegations and Nathaniel Palmer, confiding that the doctor enjoyed his 'greatest respect', suggested that the licence of Heigham Hall should not be renewed. Dr Watson, Nichols' partner, denied that the original decision to admit Holmes was inappropriate, and produced a letter from the Commissioners in Lunacy to the effect that they were satisfied that at the time of his admission Holmes had been insane. He referred to the previous occasion upon which Nichols had been consulted by the family, saying that the judgement at the time may have suggested that admission was not necessary but what happened at Mrs Bunn's cottage totally changed that judgement. At the time of his admission Holmes even described himself as morally unsound and volunteered to surrender himself to the police. As for the cure, Watson declared that, within 12 weeks, Holmes had become fit for discharge from the asylum.

There had been much speculation in the city that Dr Hull's intervention was the result of professional jealousy of Dr Ranking. And the latter gave evidence that he had invested substantially in Heigham Hall, an investment which would be lost if the licence was not continued.

Feelings ran high and the case became of national interest. The matter was reported in *The London Daily News* under the banner headline:

STARTLING REVELATION

A CLERGYMAN GUILTY OF RAPE

the Editor apparently unworried by the fact that rape had never been alleged and that Edmund Holmes had not been found guilty of anything! It seems likely that the lawyers intervened with advice because, when the paper subsequently published a letter from Nichols rejecting the allegations made by Dr Hull, it prefaced the publication with the caveat that it had excluded much of the content with the words:

> We publish the essential part of Mr Nichols' letter. Having no wish to subject either him or ourselves to a prosecution for libel, we suppress the remainder.

There are three questions to this intriguing matter. First, was the admission correct, second, if it was, how could a cure have been so swiftly completed as to allow the release of a man who did not even deny having sexually assaulted a young girl, and third, was the appointment of such a person as chaplain appropriate?

The Magistrates determined that the answer to the first question was 'yes', they kicked the second into the long grass and concluded that the appointment as chaplain was inappropriate.

At the time a huge amount of interest was generated, not just in the press, but in Parliament where the Home Secretary, Lord Palmerston, agreed to refer the matter to the Commissioners in Lunacy. The specialist press also took the matter up, with *The Lancet* carrying out its own investigation.

Despite all the rumour, the consensus opinion of the specialist press was that nothing inappropriate had occurred. *The Lancet* declared:

> we have anxiously investigated the circumstances connected with the confinement of The Revd E Holmes in Heigham Hall Asylum with the object, it is

alleged, of rescuing him from an indictment
for a criminal offence. If discredit rests
anywhere it is not with the proprietors of
the asylum, who by the open straightforward
course they have taken show that they have
nothing to fear; but rather with those who,
by their long silence and tardy accusations
have given ground for the suspicion that not
public zeal, but a less commendable motive,
has prompted proceedings.

The Journal of Psychological Medicine was even plainer in
its conclusions, referring to 'the attacks of the evil or the
attempts of unsuccessful rivals to injure an establishment
which now, for the first time in twenty years has had a
breath of scandal wafted against its walls'.

Before reaching this conclusion it too had examined
the issues. Their conclusions were that the admission was
appropriate, they too did not comment on the rapid cure,
and averred that the question of the propriety of Holmes'
appointment as Chaplain was simply a matter of opinion.

Reading the press reports of the time, which include
much detail of the meetings of the magistrates and the
investigations of the specialist press, leaves open the
opportunity to speculate on those three questions. Few
would argue that Holmes' appointment as Chaplain
was somewhat bizarre, cured or not. On the question of
the admission the balanced view would seem to be that,
whatever the motives for seeking it, the process itself
was conducted in accordance with the then prevailing
law. That was the conclusion of the Magistrates, the
Commissioners in Lunacy, The Lancet and The Journal
of Psychological Medicine. As to the appropriateness of
the decision itself note must be taken of the previous

'eccentricities' of Edmund which had led the family to consult some years earlier with Dr Nichols, and the evidence of The Revd William Wayte Andrew, whose curate Edmund had at one time been. The fact that there seems to have been a long-term belief in the locality that Edmund was insane, as expressed by both the local constable and even the mother of the alleged victim, adds weight to the presumption. That leaves unanswered (and apparently unaddressed by the contemporary investigators) the remarkable two month transformation from clinically insane to suitability for the role of chaplain. Nothing in my research of the contemporary documents shed any light on the matter, but as recently as 2015 an edition of the magazine *Psychology Today* dealing with more recent cases looked back at this case and did throw up the suggestion that such a rapid cure would have been possible had the cause of the insanity been VD. The article suggested that such a diagnosis could also explain the inconsistent and unpredictable nature of Edmund's behaviour. Could it also explain the total absence of any public conclusions on the question at the time? Holmes was, after all, both a man of the cloth and a member of a distinguished and influential family—it does not take a great leap of imagination to infer that there might have been a desire on the part of all who considered the matter to save the family further embarrassment.

As to Dr Hull's motivation for publicising his allegations, there seems to have been a wide presumption at the time that it was either dislike of Dr Nichols or professional jealousy of Dr Ranking, or perhaps a combination of both. In fact Dr Hull resigned his position at the Norfolk and Norwich Hospital shortly after the case and died just two years later.

Edmund Holmes, removed from his chaplaincy at the asylum soon found a curacy in Norwich, performing his duties to the apparent satisfaction of his Vicar.

Heigham Hall continued to be run as an asylum for a further 100 years.

A Potpourri of Parsons

The Revd Lord Frederick Townshend

Rector of Stiffkey, key figure in a clerical 'whodunnit', the strange story of the body in the coach.

On 27 May 1796 two aristocratic young brothers set out by carriage from Great Yarmouth to travel to London. The two young men were the Rector of Stiffkey and the newly returned Member of Parliament for Great Yarmouth. When their carriage arrived in London, it transpired that the newly returned Member of Parliament, was dead, having been shot in the head.

The two men were Lord Charles Townshend MP and The Revd Lord Frederick Townshend, both sons of the first Marquess Townshend. The brothers had both benefited from family patronage, Yarmouth was effectively a family seat, and the Marquess was patron of the parish of Stiffkey. The brothers had been in Yarmouth for the election.

Initially their manservants had been travelling with them, but a shortage of horses at Woodbridge meant that the brothers had to travel on alone together, their servants not arriving in London until about two hours after the discovery of the body. They were therefore unable to describe events in the later part of the journey.

One of the postillions, a Christopher Airy, was called to give evidence to the enquiry at the Public Office at

Marlborough Street the same day. He described how, at 4 o'clock that morning, he had been summoned from his bed at the Angel Inn, Ilford, on the arrival of a 'Gentleman's Chariot'. He had helped to put in four fresh horses, and then set off to drive the coach to London, accompanied by a colleague. Their instructions, from a passenger he identified as Lord Frederick, were to drive to Hanover Square. All went well to begin with and the same passenger had paid the turnpike at Stratford but, as the coach approached Mile End, Airy had heard the sound of a gun- shot, and, turning round, he saw Lord Frederick throw a pistol out of the window. Perhaps surprisingly he continued to drive, despite Lord Frederick waving his hat and beginning to shout.

When the coach arrived on the corner of Argyle Street and Oxford Street, Airy halted the coach and climbed down to ask Lord Frederick for directions. He had been told to drive the coach to the home of the Bishop of Norwich but had explained to Lord Frederick that he did not know where the Bishop lived. At this, he attested, Lord Frederick climbed down from the coach, hit him in the face, took off his coast and waistcoat, rolled up his breeches and threatened to knock him down. Airy had then opened the door of the carriage and discovered the body of Lord Charles, lying on a cushion. Soon bystanders had surrounded Lord Frederick and taken him to the watch-house.

Airy's evidence was supported by that of his fellow driver, John March, who also gave evidence that, before they left Ilford, Lord Frederick had pressed two guineas on him to be given, said the noble Lord, to any poor person, perhaps a widow with a distressed family. Such a gesture might have been seen as both generous and kind, but surely using a postilion not known to the donor as a distributor of his largesse was a little strange.

The evidence of the two postillions was followed by that of Yarmouth's former Mayor[1], the brewer Sir Edmund Lacon.

Lacon had not witnessed the circumstances of the shooting, his evidence related to the behaviour of the two Townshends, particularly leading up to their departure from Yarmouth. He claimed never to have seen a greater bond of affection between brothers than was generally the case between Lord Charles and Lord Frederick and confirmed that there had been no falling out between them at Yarmouth prior to their departure. However, he had witnessed some bizarre behaviour by both brothers that day which, in his words, amounted to 'the most indubitable symptoms of insanity'. He related that they had both 'joined in the festivity at the Election too much' and he was particularly concerned by the behaviour of Lord Charles. Both had been going about dispensing money 'lavishly and without distinction' but, on election day Charles had entered the house of his opponent[2] and only narrowly avoided being thrown out of the window. His behaviour had been such that doubts had been expressed as to whether 'he was so deranged that he could not stand the Poll'.

After the election Charles' behaviour had been strange, so strange that his friends had found it expedient to place him in a locked room the following morning having described his wild talk at dinner and his subsequent

1. Edmund Lacon was Mayor in 1792.
2. Since Townshend was elected unopposed it seems reasonable to infer that Sir Edmund was referring to a house owned by someone politically opposed to Lord Charles rather than another candidate.

repeated opening and shutting of the window shutters. The same friends determined to get him away from Yarmouth as quickly as possible and Sir Edmund had himself been so concerned that he had set out immediately to follow them by mail coach in order to warn their father, the Marquess, of their behaviour.

By this time the servants had also arrived in London. Lord Frederick's man, Parnell, gave evidence that his master had been confined for insanity two years earlier, and that he had been concerned that his master's recent behaviour might be the beginning of another such bout. Lord Charles' servant, James May, confirmed Parnell's evidence, adding that Lord Frederick had been placed in a straitjacket. He stated that, on the earlier part of the journey when the two had still been travelling with their masters, Lord Charles had been behaving in an even more deranged way, being convinced that he was being followed.

Meantime the body of Lord Charles had been taken from the coach to the premises, at 330 Oxford Street, of Mr Barnham, a chemist. Here the chemist's apprentice, a Mr Kerrison, examined the body, concluding, as he told the enquiry, that Lord Charles had been shot about two hours earlier, the pistol having been placed in his mouth prior to having been fired, a conclusion at which he had arrived as there was no damage to the teeth of the victim.

When Lord Frederick recovered some composure, he said that there had been a discussion between him and his brother during the coach journey on a 'matter of religion', that Lord Charles had then placed the pistol in his mouth himself and blown his brains out and that he, Lord Frederick, had then attempted the same action himself, but the pistol had misfired.

That same evening, an inquest was held in the pub next door to Mr Barnham's shop at 6.30 p.m. All the witnesses listed above repeated the evidence they had given to the earlier Enquiry and additional medical evidence of the location of the ball fired from the pistol. After four hours the jury retired to consider their verdict and little more than an hour later they returned a verdict 'Death occasioned by a pistol shot, but by whose hand they could not determine'.

The question remains, and will remain; was this a case of murder, suicide or even part of an uncompleted suicide pact?

Another question which might be asked is whether it was a normal occurrence for a case of possible murder to be investigated, a formal enquiry completed and an inquest held within just a few hours of a death. There seems to have been a widely held belief that Lord Charles was actually shot by Lord Frederick, who was later declared insane.

And Lord Charles' parliamentary seat? His successor was his brother-in-law, William Loftus, father of The Revd Arthur Loftus, qv.

The Revd Frank Lillingston

Rector of Salle, a 'home-schooled' Double First

Frank Lillingston had an unusual background both for a Cambridge man and for a Norfolk parson. True, his father, Claude Augustus Lillingston, had been ordained but he held no preferment other than a brief curacy, apparently becoming disillusioned with the battles between the high and low factions of the church and feeling himself unsuited for a parochial role. Lillingston senior had been born at Christchurch Mansion in Ipswich, then the home of his maternal grandfather, The Revd Charles William Fonnerau. His own father, who had been President of the Union at Cambridge in 1826, must have lived with his in-laws for many years because eight of his nine children were born at Christchurch, but in 1836 he bought another substantial Suffolk property, 'The Chantry', at Sproughton, where Claude grew up.

After Oxford and Wells Theological College, Claude dabbled unsuccessfully with sheep farming in Skye, combining this with his life's work, a scholarly tome comparing the different languages of the world which sadly, but perhaps not surprisingly, never found a willing publisher, before emigrating to Norway in 1865. There is a family tradition that he chose Norway by spinning a globe, and then, with his eyes shut, stopping the spin with his finger, having first declared that the family would settle in whichever country his finger alighted upon. It is much more likely that he chose Norway because, at the time, Norway was a cheap enough country to enable the family to live in some style, and the fishing was legendary.

Settling first in Bergen the family later moved to a tiny remote village, then accessible only by steamer, where they bought a house in which Frank was born in 1872 and, eight years later, a small estate with 500 acres of farmland, where Frank grew up. His childhood was spent in this remote area, with little to do but fish, shoot, boat, walk and immerse himself in the library his academic father had accumulated, much of which remains in the property to this day. Given the harshness of the winters, many hours must have been spent in that library. It was a very structured upbringing, in surroundings which were still fairly basic. No water was piped to the house until the 1920s and each of the rooms for the eleven children (seven sons and four daughters) was equipped with a hip bath filled every morning with water carried upstairs by some of the farmhands. There was a strict and disciplined routine to life and services were held weekly by Claude in the house.

A conventional schooling was simply not possible. Initially the children were educated by governesses imported from England, but soon Norwegian tutors were employed under the very careful eye of Claude who, with his wife, later assumed responsibility for the home schooling himself, using the older children to help educate the younger. His efforts were not in vain, three of the six sons who reached maturity gained places at Cambridge, while the less academic ones were shipped off to California where, having tried earning a living capturing rattlesnakes, one became a fruit farmer in Mexico, while the others were amongst the first to breed ostriches in Santa Barbara, both dying young.

Gaining a place for Frank at Cambridge depended heavily on patronage. He had never visited England, and, at the age of 19, he approached Pembroke College, Cambridge, writing to explain his rather unconventional educational background, and describing himself as 'very slow' at Classics and 'little better' at Mathematics. Rather than send the letter direct he sent it via a family friend, a previous member of the college, The Revd G B Thurston, asking him to endorse his application.

Thurston was hardly fulsome in his letter of support, describing Frank as 'a simple-minded lad, young for his age but withal an earnest fellow', perhaps not surprising for a boy who had lived such a sheltered life in a remote area. Rather more damning was the next sentence. 'He is not particularly bright, but very industrious, and I think he would have a very fair chance of getting a degree'.

Despite Thurston's lukewarm recommendation Frank was accepted and, after a brief stay at Thurston's Lancashire vicarage, to acclimatise himself to English social graces, he went up to Cambridge in 1891. Clearly, given his childhood, he was likely to be an unusually unsophisticated freshman and there must have been some concern about how he would cope with university life. Such concerns soon turned out to be wholly misplaced.

Given the reservations about his academic competence, what followed his admission was astonishing. In 1894 and 1895 Frank acquired a Double First in the Theological Tripos and won a string of University Prizes. He developed a special interest in the religions of the East.

He was ordained Deacon at Exeter Cathedral and took up the post of Assistant Curate at Heavitree near Exeter. His interest in the East persisted and, after ordination as a priest, he applied and was accepted for a missionary post in Delhi. Unfortunately, he was soon recognised as having too weak a constitution for such a role and instead was appointed to a Lectureship at Selwyn College, Cambridge. During his time there his published works included *The Brahmo Samaj and Arya Samaj in their bearing upon Christianity; a study in Indian theism*, recently (2015), and astonishingly, re-published as a paperback. But his health was not sufficiently robust for even an academic role and he returned to his Devon curacy before being appointed Rector of Salle in 1903, a parish within the patronage of his former college. He was by then a married man. He and his wife Elsie (nee Campbell) had five children, one of whom, Henry, followed in his father's footsteps and was the incumbent in several Norfolk parishes.

In the early years of the 20th century there was published a monthly biographical journal, called *Men of the Day*, giving brief lives of, mainly, citizens who had distinguished themselves over a lifetime of service. Frank Lillingston, at the age of just 31, featured in the September 1903 edition, lauding his Double First, his Foundation Scholarship at Pembroke and his winning of the Mason prize for Hebrew. His scholarship had clearly not gone unnoticed.

I have to declare a special interest in Frank Lillingston. He was my grandfather, my mother being his youngest child. Given the health issues that dogged his adult life it is not surprising that he died at the age of 37, just a few weeks after my mother's birth in 1909. Given both his academic achievements and his interest in the East, I like to think that, had he lived longer, he might have merited a full chapter himself.

Postscripts

The church at Salle is certainly one of Norfolk's finest, but it is also the rumoured location of the final resting place of Anne Boleyn, her remains being reputed to have been removed from the Tower Chapel following her execution. The story goes that her mortal remains were placed in a chest by her maids and buried at the Tower on the day of her execution, but that friends returned at midnight and disinterred them, removing them for reburial at Salle, which is the resting place of some of her ancestors. There are a number of contemporary and later accounts giving some credence to the story, which was also the subject of a fictional account of the transfer and reburial by Charles Dickens in the magazine *Bentley's Miscellany* in 1848.

The Norwegian property, then known as Tysse, remained in the occupation of the Lillingston family until 1967, even during the German occupation of Norway in World War 2. When I stayed there as a boy, in 1960, just two of Claude Augustus' children remained alive, my Great Uncle Claude (a widower), and his sister Edith, neither of whom had children and who were looked after by two servants who had been with the family for so many years that they were more friends than employees, and for whom the family had built as a gift a separate house in the grounds. Both farms were let to families who had farmed there for generations. When Edith Lillingston died in 1967 she left the farms to the tenants and the house to the local community, who re-named it Lillingstonheimen in honour of the family. The legacy was accepted by the community with some reservations because Edith's estate had not been large enough to establish, as she had hoped, a fund for the maintenance of what was an elderly and largely wooden structure. The community put the property to several uses over the next 50 years, while struggling financially to maintain it.

In 2018 they sold the property to a Norwegian charity established to maintain some of the country's more historic properties. It is now lived in again and there are plans to secure its future by restoring it. Care will be taken not to change its character. I revisited in September 2018 and found a near perfect Victorian time-warp. The library Claude Augustus had built up was intact, the furniture largely unchanged and the water colours of another great aunt (Laura) still covered the walls. Fortunately for the manager the charity has installed as a resident there, the house now has running water and central heating!

The Revd Augustus Beevor

Rector of Berghapton, a rather pugnacious parson.

The Revd Augustus Beevor was, like many in this book, a member of a distinguished county family. Educated at Cambridge, where, according to his obituarist, he distinguished himself by winning many prizes as a result of his literary skills.

But, as well as having such a quality, he also appears to have had rather a short fuse. On the 19 January 1801, he was tried at the Norfolk Assizes for challenging Major Edward Payne to a duel. Beevor felt that a disagreement between his father and Payne merited an apology by the latter and wrote to Payne demanding one, threatening in the absence of one to compel one 'by a mode generally used among gentlemen'. No reply was forthcoming and Beevor then publicly expressed his contempt for Payne to his face in the market place at Norwich. Found guilty, Beevor was sentenced to three weeks imprisonment, and required to provide sureties of £250 each from two others and of £500 from himself for his good behaviour for the following three years.

There is no record that he caused his sureties any concern in the next three years but he had clearly not learned from his experience because, in March 1813, he found himself in court again, this time for an assault on Daniel Turner in June 1812. Being absent from his parish he had arranged for another priest, The Revd James Carlos, to officiate for him. Carlos was a significant local landowner and also farmed the glebe lands, where Turner was one of his tenants. Turner received a message from Beevor, which indicated that he intended to remove all Carlos' stock from the glebe lands, and Turner visited the parsonage to see what it was all about. There he was greeted by Beevor who, it was said in court, 'scientifically fibbed him' hitting Turner about the head and face so that Turner screamed for help and was rescued by two other men. Beevor maintained as a defence that it was simply a 'square stand-up fight'. Beevor was again found guilty but managed to arrive at an amicable solution (presumably involving cash) with Turner as a result of which he was simply fined one shilling and discharged. What his parishioners made of the affray is not on record! He continued as Rector until his death in 1818.

The Revd Thomas Munnings

Rector of Beetley-cum-East Bilney and noted agriculturist.

Thomas Crowe Munnings was another property-owning parson, who lived at Gorgate Hall, East Dereham. Munnings was very interested in agriculture, particularly in turnips. He was obviously of an original turn of mind and distinguished himself in several ways. At the time the annual sheep shearing at Holkham was a major event attended by many distinguished and aristocratic visitors and was the scene of an exhibition of newly developed implements to reduce the labour intensity of agriculture. At the event in 1801 the machine which attracted the most interest was one invented by Munnings. It comprised a perforated box attached to 'and vertical with' the axis of a wheelbarrow, and greatly improved the process of drilling turnips. Mr Coke of Holkham was clearly impressed; he took the opportunity to announce that he would in future be giving rewards for the development of new methods of husbandry. Improvements had to be genuine. On at least one occasion he declined to make an award, saying that none of the exhibits deserved one.

Munnings' interest in turnips continued and in 1814 he was exhibiting in Norwich specimens of what he described as 'preserved turnips' where the roots could be 'earthed up' in November or December for consumption three or four months later.

His expertise was widely acknowledged and recalled by his obituarist on his death in 1827.

But not everyone appreciated Munnings. An anonymous writer, calling himself Alexander Anti-Puff of Anti-Puff Hall, published in 1810 *A Short Letter to The Revd TC Munnings*, exposing the Futility of His Pretended Agricultural Improvements. It was far from short, beginning 'in common with many people who have perused your account of some experiments on turnips, and attended to your plan for the preservation of them, I had inadvertently given in to a belief of their efficiency.........your assertions are so confident and your reasoning so plausible, as easily to seduce those who will not allow themselves the time for the patient investigation of truth'. After a few bursts of rhyme, he goes on to conclude 'Away then with your idle and expensive plans for the preservation of turnips.'

Whoever Alexander Anti-Puff was, he was persistent; the version I read was the 9th edition of the work! In fact his main target had nothing to do turnips at all, it was an attack on the tithe system. His eccentricity extended beyond his choice of alias; he dated his letter the 30 February 1810!

Alexander Anti-Puff notwithstanding, Munnings was clearly a practical man, his invention of the turnip-drill earned him an award of ten guineas and a silver medal from the Society for the Encouragement of The Arts. The

West Norfolk Agricultural Society set up a committee to investigate his claim to have found a means of preserving turnips, which they declared met with their approval, and which they recommended to their members in 1802. Munnings appears to have been one of several Norfolk clergy who devoted a proportion of the leisure time his limited duties allowed him to the improvement of local industry.

Bibliography

Anon (Alexander Anti-Puff)

A Short Letter to The Revd T C Munnings (1810)

Armstrong, C   Under the Parson's Nose (2012)

Chadwick, O   Victorian Miniature (1960)

Collier, K   Harold Francis Davidson (2004)

Collins, PT   Interviews and Recollections Volume II (1983)

Cullen, H   The Prostitute's Padre (1975)

Davage M & Musk S   No folk if you take the North Fork (2017)

Goodwin, EA   East Anglian Literature (1982)

Greaves, A   Rorke's Drift (2003)

Hartley, N   Augustus Jessopp, Norfolk's Antiquary (2017)

Jessopp, A   The trials of a country parson (1909)

Knight, I   Nothing remains but to fight (2018)

Lummis, Canon WM, MC

Padre George Smith of Rorke's Drift (1978)

Lutyens, Lady E   A Blessed Girl (1954)

Marcon, Canon WH   The Reminiscences of a Norfolk Parson (1933)

Morris, D   The Washing of the Spears (1994)

Parris, M   The Great Unfrocked (1999)

Saul, D   Zulu (2005)

Snook, Lt Col M   Like Wolves on the Fold (2010)

Thornton, T   Notes of cases in the Ecclesiastical and Maritime Courts, Volume IV (1846)

Tucker, J   The Troublesome Priest (2007)

Wade Martins, S

    A Vicar in Victorian Norfolk (2018)

Wilson, AN   After the Victorians (2006)

Index